A Century of Ra ys

around Birmingham and the West Midlands

Volume Three

1973 – 1999

85 002 enters Platform 5 at New Street from the north tunnel, 3rd October 1987. Amongst train crew, Class 85s performed well, but they were noted for being rough riders. Some drivers would habitually 'borrow' some headrest cushions from first class and put half a dozen on the cab seat to minimise the effect of the slap and the kick due to the rough ride. Two 85s have been preserved, but the remainder have been withdrawn. *(Terry Walsh)*

a personal selection by

John Boynton

INTRODUCTION

We have come a long way since the closure of Birmingham Snow Hill in 1972. A new station has risen on the ashes of the old, with fast trains to London, a re-opened route to Stourbridge and a Midland Metro tram to Wolverhampton every six minutes.

Passenger services in the West Midlands have been transformed. Trains run more frequently on every line, with seventeen new or re-opened stations added to the network. Some services have been restored after long campaigns, bringing benefits to the thousands of people who use them, whether for work or leisure.

For many years freight was in crisis, with traffic in relentless decline. That trend has been arrested, with new traffic flows developing and new locomotives to handle them.

Main line steam finished on British Rail in 1968, but steam in the West Midlands is very much alive and well, both on and off the main line, a multi-million pound industry that brings thousands of visitors to the region.

The Birmingham train builder Metro-Cammell, now Alstom, remains at the forefront of engineering design as it fulfills contracts completed with the privatised rail companies.

My other books have contained memories of those who worked on the railway in earlier years. This final volume of "A Century of Railways" includes the thoughts of some people working in today's railway industry, with their hopes for the future as one century leads into another.

John Boynton
1999

The end is nigh! Morning rush hour at the old Moor Street terminus, with arrivals from the North Warwickshire and Leamington lines. According to this photograph, Birmingham commuters on the old slam-door stock were more polite that their London counterparts, always closing the doors behind them. *(courtesy of Centro)*

47 484 'Isambard Kingdom Brunel' enters Birmingham Snow Hill, 2nd October 1987. *(courtesy of Centro)*

CONTENTS

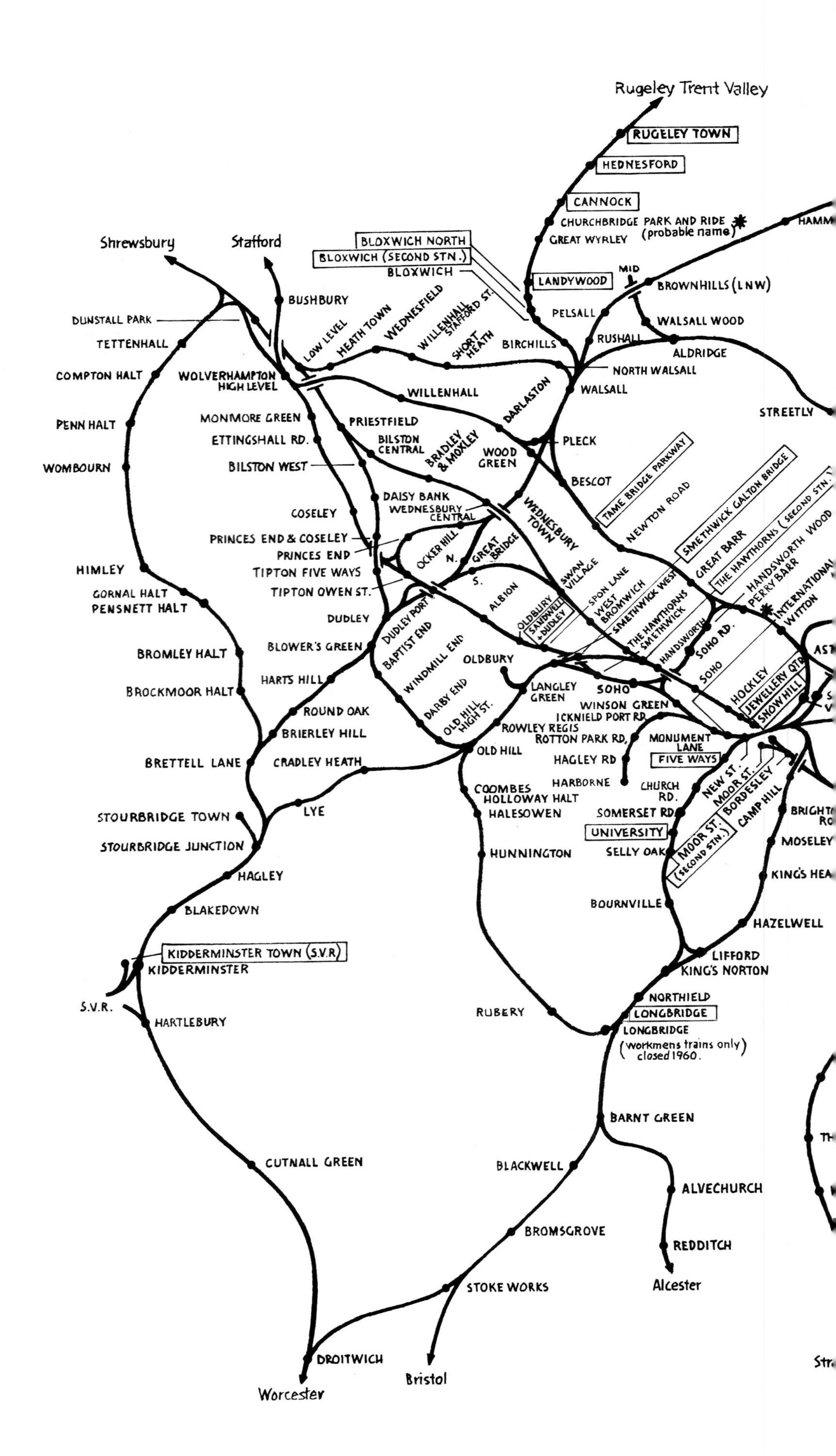

Rugeley Trent Valley
RUGELEY TOWN
HEDNESFORD
CANNOCK
CHURCHBRIDGE PARK AND RIDE (probable name)
GREAT WYRLEY
LANDYWOOD
PELSALL
MID
BROWNHILLS (LNW)
WALSALL WOOD
ALDRIDGE
STREETLY
RUSHALL
BIRCHILLS
NORTH WALSALL
WALSALL
PLECK
BESCOT
TAME BRIDGE PARKWAY
NEWTON ROAD
Shrewsbury
Stafford
BLOXWICH NORTH
BLOXWICH (SECOND STN.)
BLOXWICH
BUSHBURY
DUNSTALL PARK
TETTENHALL
COMPTON HALT
PENN HALT
WOMBOURN
HIMLEY
GORNAL HALT
PENSNETT HALT
BROMLEY HALT
BROCKMOOR HALT
BRETTELL LANE
STOURBRIDGE TOWN
STOURBRIDGE JUNCTION
HAGLEY
BLAKEDOWN
KIDDERMINSTER TOWN (S.V.R)
KIDDERMINSTER
S.V.R.
HARTLEBURY
CUTNALL GREEN
DROITWICH
Worcester
Bristol
STOKE WORKS
BROMSGROVE
BLACKWELL
BARNT GREEN
ALVECHURCH
REDDITCH
Alcester
LOW LEVEL
HEATH TOWN
WEDNESFIELD
WILLENHALL STAFFORD ST.
SHORT HEATH
WOLVERHAMPTON HIGH LEVEL
WILLENHALL
DARLASTON
MONMORE GREEN
ETTINGSHALL RD.
BILSTON WEST
PRIESTFIELD
BILSTON CENTRAL
BRADLEY & MOXLEY
WOOD GREEN
COSELEY
DAISY BANK
WEDNESBURY CENTRAL
WEDNESBURY TOWN
PRINCES END & COSELEY
PRINCES END
TIPTON FIVE WAYS
TIPTON OWEN ST.
OCKER HILL
N.
GREAT BRIDGE
S.
DUDLEY
DUDLEY PORT
BAPTIST END
WINDMILL END
DARBY END
OLD HILL HIGH ST.
BLOWER'S GREEN
HARTS HILL
ROUND OAK
BRIERLEY HILL
CRADLEY HEATH
LYE
ALBION
OLDBURY
SANDWELL + DUDLEY
SWAN VILLAGE
SPON LANE
WEST BROMWICH
SMETHWICK WEST
THE HAWTHORNS SMETHWICK
HANDSWORTH
SMETHWICK GALTON BRIDGE
GREAT BARR
THE HAWTHORNS (SECOND STN.)
HANDSWORTH WOOD
HANDSWORTH PERRY BARR
INTERNATIONAL
WITTON
SOHO RD.
SOHO
HOCKLEY
JEWELLERY QTR
SNOW HILL
OLDBURY
LANGLEY GREEN
SOHO
WINSON GREEN
ICKNIELD PORT RD.
ROWLEY REGIS
ROTTON PARK RD.
OLD HILL
MONUMENT LANE
FIVE WAYS
HAGLEY RD
HARBORNE
CHURCH RD.
NEW ST.
MOOR ST.
BORDESLEY
CAMP HILL
MOOR ST. (SECOND STN.)
COOMBES HOLLOWAY HALT
HALESOWEN
HUNNINGTON
SOMERSET RD.
UNIVERSITY
SELLY OAK
BOURNVILLE
MOSELEY
KING'S HEA
HAZELWELL
LIFFORD
KING'S NORTON
NORTHIELD
LONGBRIDGE
LONGBRIDGE (workmens trains only closed 1960.)
RUBERY

Rail Passenger Network 1900-1999

All stations and lines open to passengers during the twentieth century are shown.
Stations opened or re-opened since 1972 are boxed, eg: CANNOCK
Stations likely to be opened early in the twenty-first century are starred, eg: * WARWICK PARKWAY
Stations which closed before 1900 have their own section in the station gazetteer.

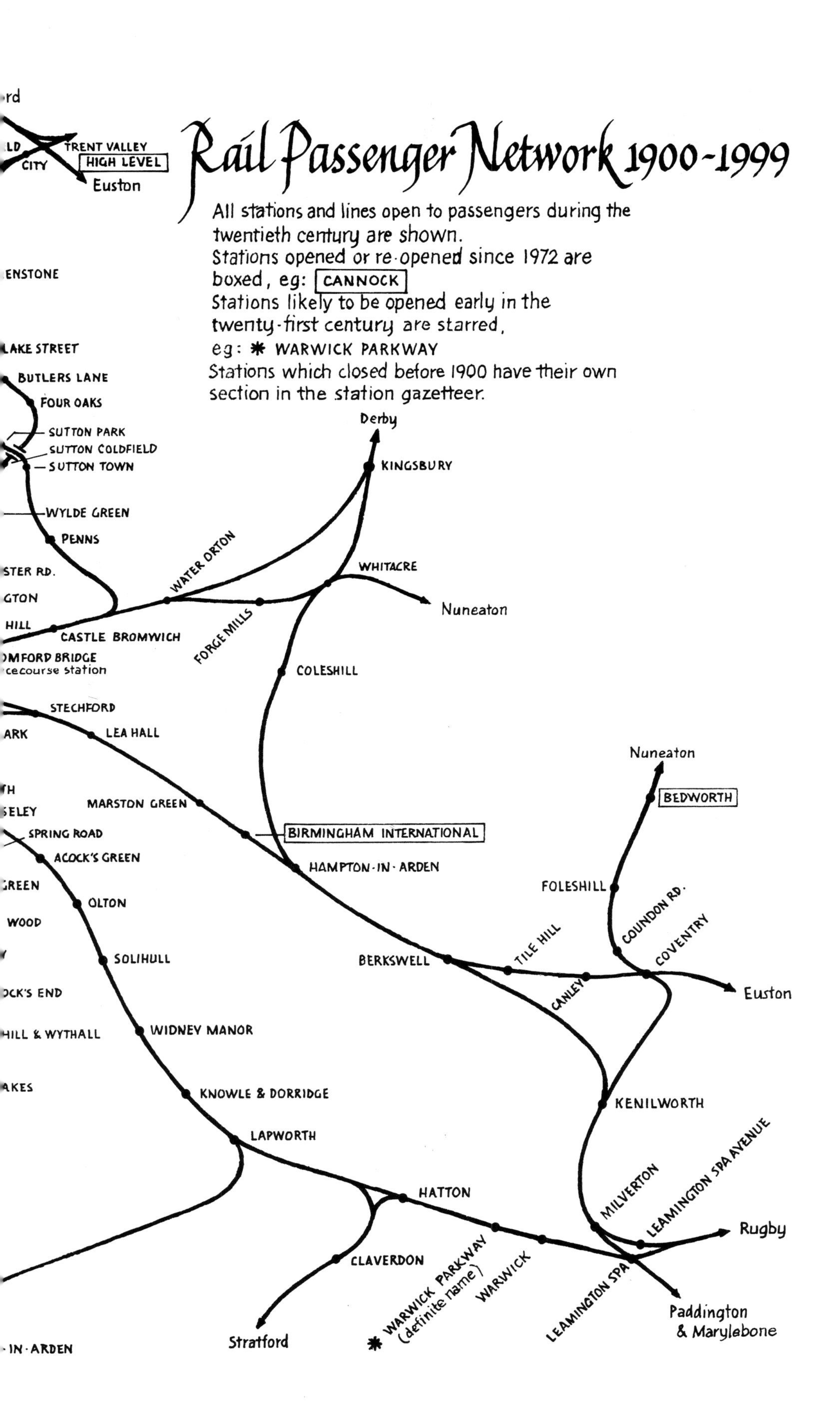

CHAPTER ONE : OUT OF THE DEPTHS, 1973-1977

[Diary : Notes : A Question of Grant Aid : Birmingham International]

Diary

1973

January 12th – WMPTE signs a £3million contract to support local rail services.

January 29th – BR announces plans for a new station at Birmingham International.

October 31st – At a meeting of the WMPTA it was agreed that, in the long term, a Kidderminster-Leamington service, via a reopened Snow Hill, should be introduced.

1974

May 6th – Start of the 1974-75 time-table. First British Rail all line time-table book, costing 50p and with 1347 pages. Birmingham-Leicester trains become hourly and more New St.-Paddington trains transferred to the old route via Oxford and Reading.

May 6th – The contraction of goods facilities continues, as Soho Pool branch closes to regular traffic. It remained open for Texaco oil trains until 1982.

1975

January 6th – Birmingham-Manchester-Greenock Freightliner service withdrawn.

October 6th – Birmingham Moor St. services improved, with four extra morning peak trains, two each from Dorridge and Shirley, which also had off-peak frequencies doubled to half-hourly.

1976

January 2nd – Severe gales thoughout the country left over 20 people dead. The many elm trees in the Midlands, killed by Dutch elm disease but still standing, were easily blown down, blocking many roads. On the railway, the overhead wires were brought down at many locations between London and Birmingham. While the disruption lasted trains ran hourly on the Paddington route, with most services in the care of Class 47 locos.

January 5th – Sidney Weighell, General Secretary of the NUR, inaugurates work on the Cross City Line by cutting the first sod at University station.

January 26th – Birmingham International station opened.

1977

May – Changes at the start of the 1977-78 timetable include diversion of Birmingham-Paddington/South Coast trains via Birmingham International and Coventry, and the Birmingham-East Anglia service was converted to loco haulage.

Notes

By 1973 the West Midlands local railway system had reached a low point. Those services which hadn't closed were simply marking time, as they had been for years.

The busiest service, between Birmingham New Street, Four Oaks and Lichfield, had not improved since it was dieselised in 1956. North of Four Oaks the line speed had been reduced from 60 to 50mph and the possibility of singling this stretch had been considered. Trains were half-hourly to Four Oaks and hourly to Lichfield. The New Street-Lichfield City journey took 41 minutes for 16 miles (average speed 23mph) and the off-peak service would have been devastated by bus competition had there been any worth speaking of. At least the train fares were purposely set lower than those of the bus and, as a sign of things to come, Wylde Green became a park and ride station in 1970 with free spaces for 45 cars. In 1972 the Lichfield trains, though not those to Four Oaks, were linked with the hourly all stations service on the Kidderminster line. Nobody used the words 'cross city' and this through service was mainly for operational convenience.

On the West Coast Main Line, electrified in 1967, things had never been better, with a fast, modern, comfortable and reliable InterCity service linking Wolverhampton, New Street and Coventry with Euston every half-hour as from March 1972. However, the local trains ran hourly as two separate services, New St.-Wolverhampton and New St.-Coventry. They did not even connect with each other and there was a gap between the westbound locals of 53 minutes! Apart from the merest handful of peak workings, the convenience of running Coventry-Wolverhampton locals as a through service had only briefly been exploited during the late 1960s. Some workings were in the hands of Class 304 emus, whose riding qualities bore a strong resemblance to those of a bouncy castle, especially on another of their happy hunting grounds, the largely jointed track of the Walsall line. The route to Walsall had been electrified in 1967, the wires terminating at just one of the station's three platforms, all that was required when the service from Birmingham was half-hourly (reduced to hourly between 1977 and 1984). Apart from an early morning emu direct to Coventry via the Aston-Stechford line, with no corresponding return train, and a summer Saturday working to Yarmouth, no other trains served Walsall.

It may seem incredible to any Birmingham rail user who does not remember the 1970s but, south of the city, Selly Oak, Bournville and Northfield were served by just four trains a day in each direction, three from the Redditch line and one from Bromsgrove. Five Ways, University and Longbridge were simply not there.

Local services not based on Birmingham barely existed. The stations between Wolverhampton and Shrewsbury 'enjoyed' a train every two hours, which took 53 minutes to cover 30 miles. This remains one of the least developed services in the region, still largely at two-hourly intervals, now generally completed in 50 minutes. The only significant new work to affect the line since 1973 has been the opening of Telford Central in 1986, long after Telford itself had begun to grow in earnest.

Coventry had lost its passenger links with Nuneaton and Leamington during the 1960s. Despite the half-hourly service to Euston, plus an hourly semi-fast to Euston via Northampton, and the hourly all stations link with Birmingham, Coventry was merely a stop on one route, just a blob on the line, like a less important Underground station devoid of connections. As was to be proved later, in a city of over 300,000 people, some of them needed to travel in other directions.

From 1957 there were regular interval services across Birmingham through Snow Hill, but these were severed in 1967. Complete closure of Snow Hill and withdrawal of its few remaining trains to Wolverhampton Low Level followed in 1972. Moor Street was the terminus for suburban trains from Leamington and Stratford-upon-Avon but they were few and unco-ordinated. Peak hour trains on the Leamington line ran to and from Moor Street, but the off-peak service terminated at New Street. No off-peak trains called at Widney Manor. North Warwickshire Line trains ran hourly to Henley and every two hours semi-fast to Stratford. Moor Street station closed after the

A Class 304 emu – still Rail Blue, non-corridor and with 1st class accommodation – arrives at Coseley with the 14.30 New Street-Wolverhampton, 28th March 1975. *(Michael Mensing)*

This photograph shows only too well what passed for the local train service between Birmingham and Redditch before the phrase 'Cross City' was invented. Bubble car 55 012 arrives at King's Norton with the 18.35 Redditch - New Street on 7th June 1975. In the background are road vehicle loading facilities. The area had earlier been occupied by Midland Railway carriage sidings; later it was the site of the Cross City Electrification Depot. *(Michael Mensing)*

arrival at 19.07 of the 18.05 from Stratford, after which the infrequent evening trains on both lines ran from New Street.

The condition of Snow Hill station deteriorated rapidly after closure. Its gaunt, sinister skeleton saw occasional use as a television and film set; by night it became a refuge for thieves, drug addicts and people just sleeping rough. An inspection carried out by British Rail surveyors in 1976 revealed that it was in danger of collapse. Large cracks had appeared in the walls, their shape and size indicating that the whole station, like a rusty glacier, had begun to move slowly down the hill. The cellar walls developed large bulges and the mortar between much of the brickwork had turned to sand. The main roof support columns were badly corroded, with many of their retaining rivets worn down to just a quarter of an inch. The demolition contract was awarded to L.E.Jones Ltd. of London, and work began with the bay platforms on 4th October 1976, moving to the main part of the station in May 1977. The site was razed by the end of that year. Developers were quick to suggest alternative uses for this prime land. They included a sports centre with an Olympic-sized swimming pool, an indoor athletics track, shops, offices, a hotel, a casino, even a heliport .....

The old station may have gone, but its main line service to Paddington, transferred to New Street, has proved more resilient, although the route has been revised on three occasions. For ten years from 1967, the exit from New Street was tortuous, briefly taking the Camp Hill line at St.Andrews Junction before leaving it at Bordesley Junction to gain the GW line at Small Heath. The Paddington trains could no longer compete with those to Euston for speed, frequency or comfort - Mark I stock was still the norm. Nobody used it for end to end journeys, but it continued to provide a reduced InterCity service for Solihull, Knowle and Leamington. Trains ran at roughly two hourly intervals. From 1972 some were diverted over the original main line, as the Western Region realised that there was considerable potential business between Birmingham, Oxford and Reading. By the 1973-74 time-table only one train in each direction was using the High Wycombe route, the 07.20 ex-New Street and the 17.40 ex-Paddington. These two workings survived until 1992. By 1974 there was an hourly service between New Street and Oxford/Reading. Some were Birmingham-Paddington trains, others served the south coast. As "Modern Railways" noted (April 1974), *"The alterations made last year, when two more Paddington-Birmingham trains were transferred from the High Wycombe route to tap traffic from Reading and Oxford, have proved successful - loadings and revenue have both shown substantial increases and it appears that new business has been attracted."*

A sample from the first all-line time-table (1974-75) gives southbound departures from New Street to Reading as follows:-

07.20 New St.-Paddington : 08.25 New St.-Paddington : 09.20 Liverpool-Poole : 10.25 New St.-Paddington : 11.20 Newcastle-Poole : 12.25 New St.-Paddington : 13.25 New St.Paddington, etc.

There were easy connections, cross-platform wherever possible, at New Street. For example, the 09.20 to Poole arrived at 09.05, while a Leeds-Paignton service arrived and departed (09.10-09.15) alongside. The 10.25 to Paddington was met by the Manchester-Cardiff (arr.10.07 dep.10.20) and the Leeds-Penzance "Cornishman" (10.10-10.15) which more obviously connected with each other.

The commercial potential for an hourly Bristol-New Street-Sheffield service had been realised for some years; the useful link with Reading and the south coast was a natural progression, the strengthening of another spoke in New Street's wheel as the hub of the InterCity network. Contrary to original expectations, the role of the Paddington route, at least the northern half of it, had been redefined rather than downgraded. The trains themselves, for long the preserve of "Western" diesel hydraulics, were hauled by Class 50s from May 1976, although a few Westerns were pressed into service after that date.

The opening of Birmingham International in 1976 was followed in May 1977 by a further alteration to the route of the Birmingham-Paddington/South Coast trains although, as explained in this chapter's section on that station, their time-tabling was eccentric at first.

West Coast electrification to Glasgow was completed in 1974. In the meantime, British Rail had tried to make the West Midlands-Glasgow journey easier with tighter, faster schedules, possible only by double heading the trains north of Crewe to lift them over Shap and Beattock at reasonable speeds. Thus the 1973 'Midland Scot' left New Street at 08.15 and, splitting at Carstairs in the time honoured way, arrived in Glasgow at 13.30 and Edinburgh at 13.35. With electrification however, the same train left New Street and 08.10 and arrived in Glasgow at 12.33 and Edinburgh at 12.39. The number of through daytime Birmingham-Glasgow trains doubled from two to four. Additionally the new London-Inverness 'Clansman' called at Coventry, New Street and Wolverhampton. Not surprisingly, passenger loadings between Birmingham and Glasgow/ Edinburgh, for a four week period in August-September 1974, showed a 116% increase over the same period for 1973. With the 1974 electrification, the Bristol-Birmingham-Newcastle sleeper was diverted to Glasgow and Edinburgh instead. Its passengers had the benefit of Mark III sleeping cars from September 1983 and the service was later extended to/from Plymouth, which meant a northbound departure from New Street at an unattractive 01.30. The train ceased to serve Birmingham in 1991 and was withdrawn completely in 1995.

During the 1970s the route between the West Midlands, Leicester and East Anglia experienced growth, but starting from a very low base indeed. In 1973 there were just twelve trains a day between Birmingham and Leicester, irregularly spaced with gaps of up to two hours. Five went through to Norwich, two to Cambridge and one to Nottingham. This is a far cry from today, with two trains an hour to Leicester, hourly trains to Cambridge and two an hour to Nottingham via Derby.

In 1973 the Norwich trains were sometimes in the hands of Swindon Cross Country dmus, but too often this duty was left to high density suburban dmus, as were all the Leicester workings. The London Midland and Eastern regions were aware that the service was totally inadequate. They used some of their limited supply of spare rolling stock to effect an improvement. Birmingham-Leicester became hourly in 1974, with an increase to six trains to Norwich, which took between 4 hours 4 minutes and 4 hours 56 minutes for the 175 miles (less than 4 hours today in a Class 158 dmu, even with the usual change and wait of up to 20 minutes at Peterborough). Completion of electrification between Kings Cross and Royston in 1977 released some Class 31 locos, which were replaced by emus. These locos, together with some surplus Mark I stock made up into five, six or seven-car rakes, provided a much enhanced Birmingham-Norwich service. (It was not quite the first time that diesel loco-hauled trains had been used on this line. During the 1960s the Sunday evening rush at New Street saw the busiest train of the week, a motley rake of carriages bound for Peterborough, with a Class 25 or 26 at its head.) Use of the 31s, despite some low line speeds, notably 50mph between Manton Junction and the East Coast Main Line and 30mph through Whitacre, breached the four hour barrier for Birmingham-Norwich for the first time. Reversal at Ely was avoided by use of the sharply curved freight link

The stamping ground of Kings and Castles no more, a derelict Snow Hill, together with the south power box, March 1972. *(R.G.Amott)*

Desolation as a bubble car for Wolverhampton waits in the gaunt remains of Birmingham Snow Hill, Thursday 2nd March 1972, two days before the end of service. The platform seat had seen happier days in the station buffet. *(R.G.Amott)*

56 074 "Kellingley Colliery" at Brickyard Crossing between St.Andrew's and Landor St. junctions, 3rd August 1983. In the background is the Euston line between Grand Junction and Adderley Park. The grill covers the intake for the cab air conditioning. The loco was based at Healey Mills. *(Terry Walsh)*

between Ely West and North junctions, so by-passing the station. Ely and Cambridge passengers had smart connections at Peterborough or March. These trains even attempted West Coast Main Line connections at Nuneaton, an early reminder that it is not always necessary for passengers to be processed through New Street!

The mid-seventies saw some interesting shifts in motive power. Diesel hydraulic 'Hymek' locos had been used as bankers on the Lickey Incline. Somewhat underpowered, they had to work in threes to do any good, little more effective than the Jinties of old. They were replaced in 1973 by Class 37s, familiar for the heavy-duty double-bass roar of their engines. They banked in pairs – impressively.

In 1974 orders were placed for 60 new heavy freight locomotives *"urgently needed for the haulage of heavy coal trains following the government's decision to concentrate on coal extraction in its national fuel policy."* ("Modern Railways", November 1974). Less than thirty years later, that policy most definitely sounds as though it belongs to another century! The locos, built 1976-84, became the Class 56 Type 5 Co-Co, the first 30 of which were built by Electroputere at Craiova, Romania, as sub-contractors for Brush. During 1976 mid-life refurbishment began at Crewe for the 500-strong Class 47. "Modern Railways" (April 1976) correctly predicted that, *"This mid-life attention will ensure that the class will operate for at least a further 15 years - well into the late 1990s"*.

As new coaching stock was introduced on Wolverhampton-Euston trains, earlier types of electric loco, Classes 81-85, had to be found other duties because they were not compatible with the train heating systems of the Mark IId and subsequent designs. Such locomotives had virtually disappeared from this route by May 1976, when Mark IIIs began appearing, but were still to be seen hauling pre-IId stock on the northern leg of the SW-NW route, when traction was changed at New Street.

Insofar as stock for local trains was concerned, 1st March 1976 saw a refurbished high density Class 116 dmu, the first in the West Midlands, undertake an acceptance tour of local lines for the WMPTE. Refurbishment also included the new white livery, smart when fresh but highly impractical. Also at this time, four new 4-car Class 312 emus (sub class 312/2) were delivered from York works to operate PTE local trains between Birmingham and Coventry. They were in Rail Blue, never attaining all-white status. Other members of the class, including the 312/0s which operated between Kings Cross and Royston, were regarded as outer suburban units and had a maximum speed of 90mph. The 312/2s were limited to 75mph.

The continuing contraction of freight services was a depressing feature of the 1970s. The switch from rail to road continued unabated. Long established facilities disappeared. Soho Pool closed to general freight in 1974; Cadburys ceased to use rail in 1976. When Cadburys rail traffic had been at its peak, during the 1920s and 30s, four trains a day were dispatched from

50 021 "Rodney" passes Adderley Park school, if not yet the station, with the 10.10 New Street-Paddington service, via Birmingham International and Coventry, 6th December 1986. The land in the foreground is the site of Adderley Park goods yard, which handled coal and general merchandise. *(John Whitehouse)*

"Each a glimpse and gone for ever" – a scene that has since utterly changed. The eastern end of Washwood Heath Yard is now dominated by the viaduct of the Heartlands Spine Road. Large logo 31 143 shunts at the yard throat, whilst on the main line 31 448 passes with the 18.30 Birmingham-Norwich train. 25th April 1988. To the left is the Nuffield Works, now the Leyland Daf works, Metro-Cammell to the rear in the mist. The six sidings alongside the main line were officially the 'Birmingham Sidings, but locally called the 'Dugout', because they were 'dug out' after the main yard. *(John Whitehouse)*

the works. Even the Freightliner network, of which Dr.Beeching had such high hopes, was not immune. Several routes closed at the beginning of 1975, including Birmingham-Greenock.

Another attempt to promote freight was the establishment of a network of fast air-braked trains, aimed at securing more wagonload traffic. Given the brand name Speedlink by the Chairman of the BRB, Peter Parker, on 13th September 1977, of the 29 daily services running by then, three started from Birmingham - to Newcastle, Manchester and March. There were prospects for new links between Birmingham and Sheffield, and also with London via Leicester. Initially Speedlink met with much success, operating at a profit and with a reputation for reliability. During the late 1980s all rail freight suffered a steep decline in fortune, a downward spiral from which it seemed impossible to escape. There was no equivalent of grant aid for freight services to see them through periods of recession, and not even the most modern air-braked wagons had either the vote or any political influence. The entire Speedlink network was axed in the early 1990s, a victim of government 'economies'.

British Leyland was booming during much of the 1970s, due in no small measure to the success of their Allegro cars, of which Longbridge could produce 4,000 a week. BL brought body panels from the Pressed Steel Fisher plant at Swindon by rail, which generated nine trains a week. They returned to Swindon with spares and 'completely knocked down' cars for export in kit form. The trains were hauled by Class 47s and were routed via Cheltenham. Longbridge was - and remains - a major traffic flow for rail. Just up the line, the former carriage sidings at Kings Norton had been adapted to serve as a rail loading point for British Leyland vehicles. Elsewhere in the West Midlands, the opportunities for the motor industry to use rail were limited. The Coventry Loop Line had opened in 1914 specifically to serve nearby industries. In August 1977 a short-lived Freightliner depot opened on the loop at Gosford Green, to serve the Chrysler plant. One train a day ran between Coventry and another Chrysler plant at Linwood, Scotland. Chrysler had run company trains between Coventry and Linwood in earlier years. They ceased, and Chrysler briefly used road for the whole journey, then reverted to train between Linwood and Dudley Freightliner Terminal, for road haulage to Coventry.

Another major motor manufacturer is Land Rover at Solihull. In 1974 this was simply Rover and described as "uncomfortably remote" from a railway. As the century closes the Rover Group has plans for a rail link to connect its Lode Lane plant with the main line near Birmingham International. The extra traffic, though welcome, will create problems for an already overcrowded railway and it will be interesting to see how the parties involved attempt to square this particular circle.

Shunter 08 742, brake van in tow, passes the ex-Midland Railway box at Longbridge East, surrounded by the motor works, 3rd May 1978. The works area to the left of the track was levelled during 1998. This end of the former Halesowen Railway is still awaiting a passenger service to Frankley, talked of and seen as desirable – by Centro and others – almost since the Cross City service began.

(Michael Mensing)

A 2-6-0 freight loco of the 4300 Class, 7332, heads a southbound freight on the goods avoiding lines through Stourbridge Junction, 2nd June 1962. This area now forms part of the station car park. *(Brian Moone)*

A Question of Grant Aid

The large scale closures of the Beeching era were a crude attempt to prune unprofitable parts of the system in the naive belief that this would somehow make the rest more prosperous. 'Loss-making' lines included suburban routes in all the major conurbations, but any government contemplating their closure in any quantity would be taking a huge risk. The few voters in rural Cumberland could be ignored; the massed commuters of the Home Counties could not. Once this had sunk into the political consciousness, the social benefits of 'unprofitable' lines were recognised in law.

As a result of the Transport Act of 1968, two things happened. Passenger Transport Authorities (PTAs), were set up in the major conurbations outside London (the capital had its own unique transport problems which no one was yet willing to tackle). All loss making rail services, whether in the PTA areas or not, were to receive financial support from central government. The money was awarded in advance, for a period of one or two years, line by line. This 'grant aid', as it was called, was no guarantee against closure, but it did help secure the future of many services. In the West Midlands PTA area, station and line closures ceased after 1972, apart from Smethwick West, which was a special case.

Original WMPTA boundary stations were Codsall, Shenstone, Water Orton, Hampton, Knowle, Danzey, Redditch, Bromsgrove and Hagley. The present reduced boundary came into effect with local government reorganisation in 1974. The PTA and its Executive (WMPTE, now named Centro) carried out a comprehensive study of the bus and train services in its area and published its Passenger Transport Development Plan in November 1972. So far as rail was concerned, there were two categories of service. Category A was reckoned to have a valuable role in the efficient movement of large numbers of people and should be permanently supported. Category B was reserved for routes where the trains were not well used, the losses were heavy and the potential for future development was minimal. Such lines were not thought to have a long term future and were not to receive long term investment. The Birmingham-Walsall, Birmingham-Wolverhampton locals and Stourbridge Junction-Stourbridge Town services were Category B. All the others were in Category A, even the minimalist service to Redditch, which attracted just 200 passengers a day, less than half that on Saturdays. The Plan was astute enough to recognise the potential of the Redditch line, especially if linked across the city with the Lichfield line. New stations were to be provided where there was a real need, at Five Ways, University and Longbridge. Mention was made of electrification, plus the line's own tunnel and deep level platforms at New Street.

The Plan expressed concern about lack of capacity between New Street and Coventry, a problem still to be addressed. On the Kidderminster line, two thirds of commuters came into Birmingham from Stourbridge or beyond. A 250 space car park was planned for Stourbridge Junction, where parking had been confined to the station approach road.

In Category B, New Street-Wolverhampton local services were not, in the view of the WMPTA, fully co-ordinated with other services along the line and apparently this caused them to be given temporary grant aid while *"discussion between the parties"* continued. The Walsall service was a heavy loss-maker, with *"no known new projects for development in the area served which could generate more traffic"*. The Plan acknowledged the existence of the M6 and the recently completed A34M Aston Expressway as a perceived threat to the viability of the Walsall line (sic) but noted that although the Expressway had only been open for a few months it was already heavily congested during the peaks. *"Accordingly, the Authority and Executive are to continue financial support on a temporary basis"*. Thus, by a curious logic, the motorway apparently helped the Walsall line survive its leanest years. It was intended to replace the Stourbridge Town shuttle with a bus; happily the 'Town Car' still functions.

The Authority signed an agreement with the British Railways Board on 12th January 1973 whereby the WMPTE would take responsibility for local rail services within and a little beyond its area to the 'natural terminus' for each line. The PTE would decide fares and service frequency; British Rail would operate the trains on their behalf. The PTE would pay each line's grant aid to BR. Central government would pay 80% of the grant to the PTE, which would raise the remaining 20% by a precept on the rates. The government could withhold its 80% share from the PTE if it did not approve of the services provided.

These dry financial arrangements were the start of many years' successful co-operation between the Authority and British Rail, during which services on all PTE lines expanded and improved. Total grant aid payable to British Rail for 1974 was £81million. West Midlands local lines were to receive £1,446,000, shared as follows (figures in 000s) - Birmingham to Worcester via Kidderminster (223), to Lichfield (95), to Stratford via Henley (178), to Coventry and Rugby (274), to Wolverhampton and Stafford (95), to Leicester and Derby (220), to Leamington (204), to Stratford via Lapworth (49), to Worcester via Bromsgrove (13), to Redditch (95).

The Development Plan made much of integration between bus and rail and this policy took a big step forward in October 1975. Peak hour services to Dorridge and Shirley were improved, and the off peak trains doubled to half-hourly. Bus services were modified to connect with trains at Shirley, where a bus turning circle was provided. An experimental dial-a-ride bus began connecting with trains at Dorridge. Of wider benefit was the extension of the Travelcard, already in use on the buses, to the local rail network. A four-week card (with passport type photo), valid on all trains and buses, cost just £8. A weekly card was £2.25. Child equivalents were £3 and £1. Even in 1975 this was cheap, the best value ticket of any PTE in the country.

It was WMPTE policy to pitch fares at this low level to generate more passengers and encourage a shift away from the private car. On official estimates, over 3,000 commuting motorists abandoned their cars for the train and bus within six months of the Travelcard's introduction. However, the Department of Transport stated that WMPTE fares were too low and threatened to cut the general rate support grant in direct proportion to the extra grant required by the rail services, unless the fares were raised. These London-based politicians were blessed with a vision that seemed incapable of seeing any merit whatsoever in the provision of inexpensive public transport. The Department issued a directive to the PTE, which was thus compelled to increase its fares in January 1977. The £8 Travelcard remained, but other fares were raised by an average of 23%, with a further rise of 25% in September 1977, well above the rate of inflation.

Despite rising fares, a survey carried out for the PTE during 1977 showed increases in the use of local rail lines averaging 36% over a two year period. The North Warwickshire Line had an increase of 51%. During the same year, sale of travelcards exceeded 100,000 for the first time. In May, the PTE published the first ever bus and rail time-table booklet for the West Midlands, although it only covered Birmingham, Solihull and Sutton Coldfield.

There were as yet no new stations. Clearly some were planned as part of the Cross City Line. Others would be needed on the Jewellery Line, which opened in 1995. PTA approval for such a line, when it agreed in principle to through trains between Kidderminster and Leamington via a reopened Snow Hill, was given at a meeting held on 31st October 1973, barely eighteen months after final closure of the old Snow Hill. Be that as it may, the first new station in the PTE area would be large, impressive - and not really meant for local traffic.

Stourbridge Town shorn of its platform canopy, bubble car at the ready, 3rd December 1977. *(Malcolm Keeley)*

When the Aston Expressway was due for repair both nearside lanes were to be closed. The photographer obtained permission from the City Engineer to travel along this urban motorway (A38M) in pedestrian mode, resulting in fine photographs from unusual vantage points on a hot clear day, 7th May 1987. Between metal bashing in the foreground and Villa Park in the distance, a Class 312 emu provides a Walsall-New St. service along the Grand Junction line, opened in 1837. To the rear of Halliday's, near the horizon, is ICI Kynoch's at Witton. *(John Whitehouse)*

Seen from the Aston Expressway a Class 116 dmu, recently transferred from the Cardiff Valley lines – judging by the red end whiskers – heads towards Spaghetti Junction with a Cross City service to Lichfield, 7th May 1987. *(John Whitehouse)*

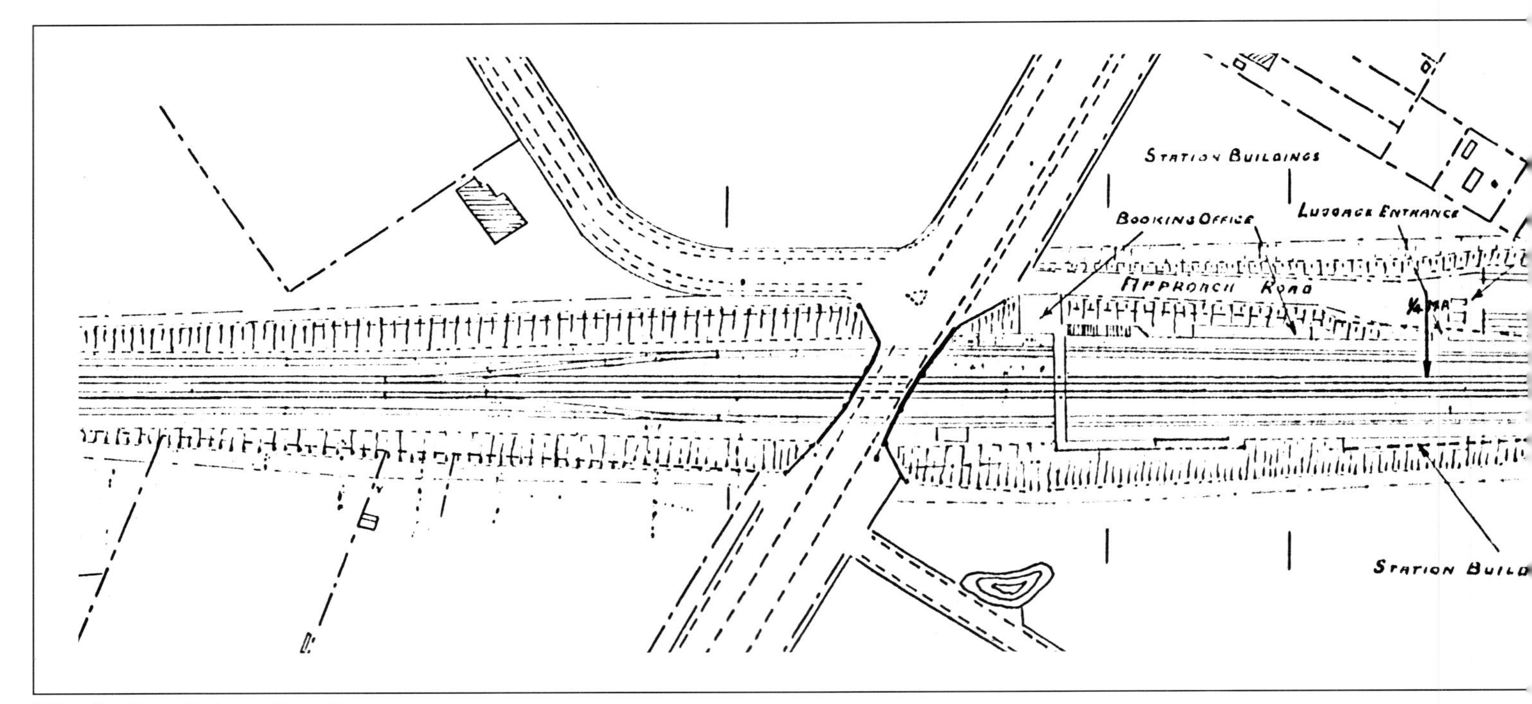

Birmingham International

Proposals for a station at Bickenhill date back to 1937. The Chief Engineer's Office of the LMS (based at St.Pancras Chambers, the former Midland Hotel which had closed its doors to guests just two years earlier) drew up plans for a station with two 500 foot platforms, on the north side of the bridge that carried the A45 Coventry Road over the railway. It would have been a half mile walk from the centre of Bickenhill, along Church Lane and across the A45, which was then a single carriageway relatively free of traffic. The station was to be fully staffed, with a small three road goods yard complete with weighbridge. The existing cutting would be widened, as the station platforms were to be on long loops, with the through running lines remaining on their existing alignments. The LMS intended to quadruple the Birmingham-Coventry line, which is why the layout took this form. Bickenhill was designed purely as a local station, as the platform lengths indicate. Had it been built it would have been the nearest point on the railway to the terminal buildings for Elmdon Airport, which opened in July 1939. It is interesting to speculate how airport and station would have developed, separately and in relation to each other, had not the Second World War intervened.

Birmingham International, half a mile north of the Coventry Road, was also known as Bickenhill in the planning stages. This was just a convenient label until a more suitable name could be chosen. Its primary purpose was to serve the National Exhibition Centre (NEC) and the airport, so its name would have to reflect this.

The NEC was the first purpose built exhibition complex in the country, begun as a joint venture between Birmingham Corporation and Birmingham Chamber of Commerce & Industry. It was designed with an exhibition space area of 1 million square feet over six halls, plus a conference centre and two hotels although, rather like Heathrow Airport, it has grown more or less continuously ever since it opened. The green field site was chosen because of its accessibility by road, rail and air, but in 1972, when construction began, accessibility was more potential than real. There was no station, indifferent road access compared with today, and the airport had its back to the site. The first piece of the NEC's transport jigsaw to be put into place was the station, 106¾ miles from Euston, bordered on the east by the 310 acre NEC site, with airport land to the west.

The station's estimated contruction cost of £3.6million (1973) had risen to £5.9million on completion. Work began in March 1974 and the station, almost complete, was opened on 26th January 1976, just too late for the first exhibition. This had occurred on the weekend of January 3rd-4th, a 'fun event' curtain raiser in four halls, with musical entertainment, vintage vehicle displays, etc. Most people came just to see the NEC itself, 100,000 on the Saturday, an estimated 150,000 on the Sunday, causing gridlock on the surrounding roads and forcing thousands of motorists to abandon their journeys and head for home instead.

During construction of the station most trains continued running, at reduced speed through the middle of what was a building site, although there were Sunday diversions. In the early stages the main contractor, A.Monk & Co. of Warrington, erected a 20 foot high wire mesh fence to protect the workforce from the trains and the catenary. A name was agreed for the new station - *"After consideration of 200 suggestions from the public as a result of local press publicity, it has been jointly agreed between British Rail, the Metropolitan County Council, the Passenger Transport Executive and the National Exhibition Centre that the station should be known as Birmingham International"* (Modern Railways, September 1974).

The station has five 1,000 foot long platforms, each capable of accommodating a 13 coach train. There was (and is) sufficient land to extend the platforms to 16-coach length and to add another island platform on the NEC side, should the need arise. There are small waiting rooms on each platform, which are otherwise largely featureless. Most station amenities are carried on a concrete deck above the platforms. The concourse gives access to the ticket office and travel centre, the bookstall, a cafeteria and a pleasant open plan waiting area close to the stairs leading down to the platforms. The original ticket barriers have been removed. There is an up escalator from the road entrance to the concourse but, as at New Street, there is no down equivalent. A wide covered walkway links the station directly with the NEC. The external ribbed steel cladding is in the same style as the adjacent exhibition halls.

Birmingham International was the first InterCity station on a new site since London Marylebone in 1899. When it opened, only two morning peak trains to Euston called here, the 07.18 and

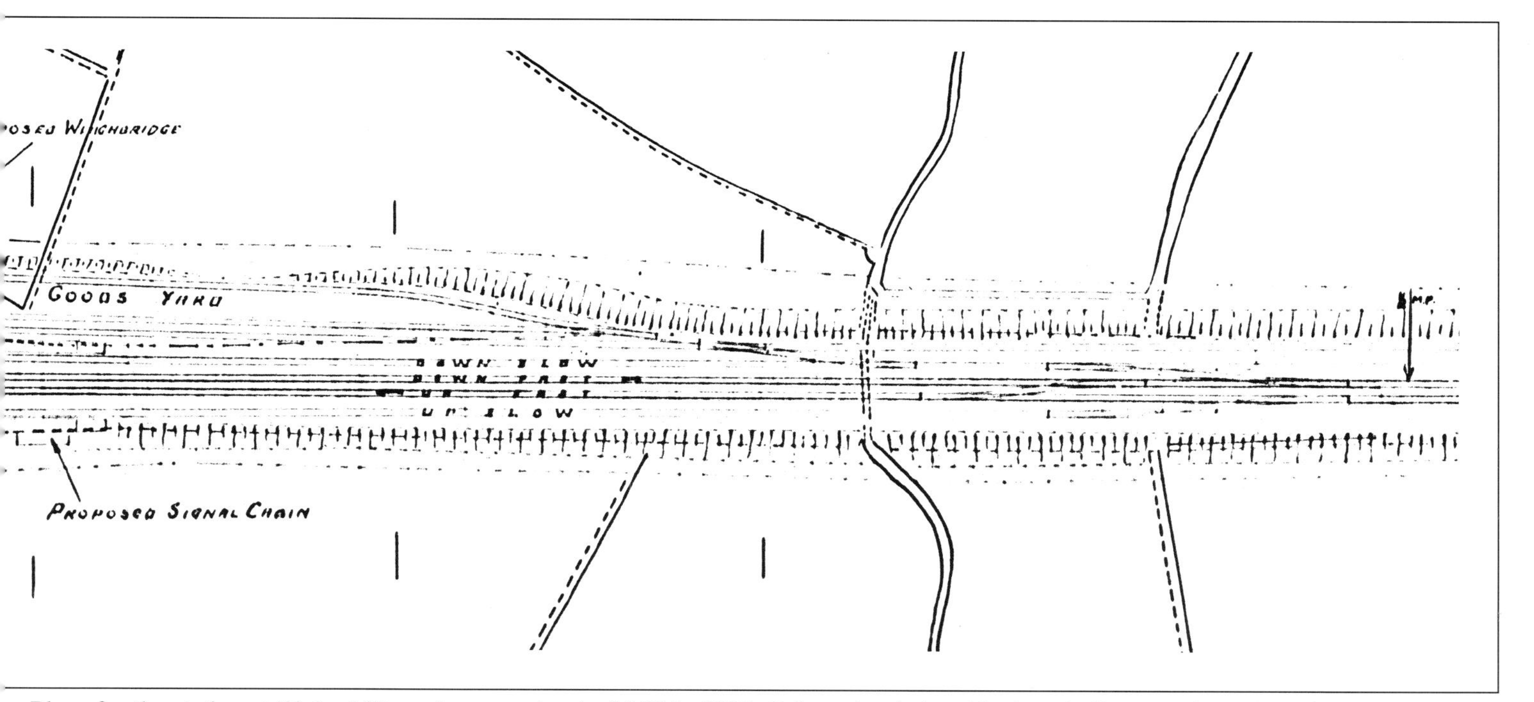

Plans for the station at Bickenhill, as drawn up by the LMS in 1937. Orientation is 'upside down', Coventry is to the left, Birmingham to the right. *(courtesy of Railtrack)*

08.15 from New Street; the 06.48 and 07.48 called at Hampton-in-Arden, the 08.48 omitted both. All Euston trains from the 09.18 onwards called, with a journey time of 80 minutes. There was a similar evening peak pattern in the down direction. Between 1977 and 1980 a few peak InterCity trains called at both Hampton and International, four minutes apart, a gross waste of brake fluid on this congested stretch of line! Hampton had become the substitute 'InterCity' station for the Solihull area in 1967, but reverted to a purely local station with effect from May 1980. When International opened, the hourly New St.-Coventry locals were supplemented by an hourly New St.-International shuttle. These trains did not load well and were later withdrawn. International is an important station for long distance travellers but not the natural terminus for any purely local service.

Its first big test came when the Motor Show was held at the NEC for the first time between 20th and 29th October 1978. The show occupied six halls and was twice as big as the previous one, held at Earl's Court in 1976. The normal service from Euston was doubled to four trains per hour before 13.00, with this intense flow reversed after 16.00. The special Awayday fare of £7 included admission to the show (£5 at weekends, £15 for a family of four). Other long distance trains ran direct from Liverpool and Manchester, using the Aston-Stechford line, and from the Reading line. The locals between Birmingham and Coventry, normally hourly, were doubled. There were some direct local specials from Walsall, using the Aston-Stechford line. Most WMPTE local stations were normally closed on Sundays, but they were opened for the two Sundays of the show and provided with at least an hourly service. It was possible to buy a combined train/show ticket at a discount from all local stations. The Birmingham-Coventry line was at saturation point, with all trains trickling along on single yellow signals for much of the day. With the five platforms and footbridge link to the halls continually thronged with people, the station came into its own. 908,000 people visited the show, about 250,000 arriving by rail. How pleasantly different from the 1998 Motor Show, when there were very few extra trains from Euston and none whatsoever from anywhere else, including New Street. People reaching the show by rail often had to travel in dangerously overcrowded trains and, as they attempted to make their way home again, staff at International were compelled to make announcements warning that the platforms were becoming so overcrowded they they might have to be closed. Did Virgin Trains miss a market opportunity here?

Whilst International is very busy during public exhibitions, it has two other major roles, as a parkway station and as a link to the airport. There is a large surface car park and the station can now be reached easily from the A45 and Junction 6 of the M42, a motorway that did not exist in 1976.

Extra passengers were attracted with the diversion of some Birmingham-Paddington/South Coast trains via International, Coventry and the Coventry-Leamington line, with effect from May 1977. At first though, each day's trains to New Street all took the new route until the 11.50 from Paddington, after which they reverted to the Solihull line. In the other direction, all trains took the old route until the 14.38 from New St. to Paddington. Such a lopsided service meant that some passengers could not return on the same day to their starting station without considerable inconvenience. Once this imbalance was addressed the service began to flourish. All InterCity trains between Birmingham and Reading now use the route via International, which is also (summer 1999 time-table) the starting point for some long distance services, eg; 06.40 and 10.13 to Manchester, 10.16 to Newcastle, 10.31 to Edinburgh, etc.

The 1977 re-routing to serve International meant re-opening the 9-mile single track Coventry-Leamington freight line to passenger traffic. As early as 1975 the Railway Development Association was calling for re-opening of this line as an addition to the local network – *"It is claimed that a regular hourly service would be of particular benefit to the growing population of Kenilworth, as well as providing the 335,000 inhabitants of Coventry with important connections into services from Leamington to Stratford, Reading and Southampton"* (Modern Railways, June 1975). Today there is roughly one train an hour, although the line remains single track and is almost at capacity. Kenilworth is still stationless.

A busy Sunday scene at Kenilworth's distinctive station, 1st October 1961. At left, a three-car Metro Cammell dmu arrives from New Street with a service for Coventry. Due to main line electrification work in the Coventry area, this train ran via the Berkswell direct line and reversed at Kenilworth. The two-car Metro Cammell dmu in the station forms a Leamington-Coventry service. Kenilworth closed in 1965, and the station approach site is now given over to housing, but a station is needed to serve this growing town. In addition, doubling between Coventry and Leamington would relieve congestion on this important link line. *(Michael Mensing)*

Birmingham International station has always had a busy taxi rank and a row of bus stops. The primary purpose of the buses here is not to provide a service to Birmingham or Coventry – people can simply stay on the train – but to areas which are not served by rail. The station opened with feeder buses to the airport terminal, but in 1984 they became unnecessary for a while. Traffic at the airport had been growing relentlessly and by the late 1960s the augmented 1939 terminal buildings were finding it increasingly difficult to cope. There were, of course, domestic and European routes, but nothing beyond. Birmingham was desperate to secure at least one North Atlantic route, but needed facilities to match. The runway was extended and a new terminal provided at the other side of the airfield, much nearer International station and the NEC. The new terminal at Birmingham International Airport was officially opened, with a visit from Concorde, on 31st May 1984.

From 7th August, there was a novel link between the terminal and the station, provided by Maglev, two driverless cabins (plus a spare which could be coupled to one of the others) on a 650 metre long concrete viaduct. They worked by magnetic levitation, floating a few millimetres above the 'track' and giving a smooth effortless ride, linking the station concourse and the airport departures area without the need for stairs or a lift, an important consideration for passengers with luggage. Access was by a double door, which matched doors in the screen on each platform edge. Maglev was a small but important part of the transport jigsaw at the airport. During construction a large billboard proclaimed *"A First for Britain. The world's first operational magnetic suspension transport system will be open here to the public in the spring of 1984"*. Built by Metro-Cammell, the 8-tonne cabins had seating for 6 and standing room for 36. As 'prototypes' they were expensive to operate and maintain, but this was offset by the perceived potential for this type of transport in similar situations. After initial teething troubles they ran successfully. Maglev could operate at two minute intervals and carry 2,600 people in each direction every hour, all free of charge. The Birmingham system was seen as a testbed which could continue to develop this specialist type of transport and generate orders for the manufacturer. However, as airport traffic grew further, a second terminal, Eurohub, was built but an extension of Maglev into the new terminal was not incorporated at the design stage. It closed on 19th June 1995, allegedly because it had become costly to obtain spare parts. At the time of writing it remains in place, unused. Transfer between station and airport is now by bus, far less convenient whichever yardstick is used. More recently, it seems virtually certain that Line 2 of the Midland Metro, from the city centre to the airport, and for which Parliamentary powers have now lapsed, will never be built. It could have had stops at the airport and station, and within the NEC site. Thus Maglev and Metro Line 2 were both victims of that persistent virus, Planners' Folly.

The Maglev was a piece of the transport jigsaw that was placed in position - it worked well but was abandoned by the shortsighted. The Metro line was one piece of the jigsaw which never even left the box. There was another. This from the pages of 'Modern Railways' (December 1977) – *"The two main developments in British Rail's Motorail network in 1978 are likely to be new terminals at Harwich and Birmingham International"*. Whatever happened to that excellent idea?

Class 86/0 No.86 045, with a rake of Mark III stock (except for the brake van and buffet car) form the 11.40am (Su O) Euston-Wolverhampton, 20th October 1974. To the rear is Birmingham International station and the National Exhibition Centre, newly emerging from the mud.
(Michael Mensing)

A four-car Class 310 emu, with wrap around cab windows, leaves Birmingham International with the 12.50 New Street-Coventry service on 26th February 1977.
(Michael Mensing)

A Coventry-Birmingham Class 310 emu pauses at Hampton-in-Arden, 29th January 1973. The storyline accompanying this picture correctly predicted that when the newly announced station at Bickenhill (Birmingham International) opened, Inter City trains would cease to call here. *(courtesy of Birmingham Post & Mail)*

47 650 is seen at Wolverhampton on 1st May 1989. The black metal horse in the foreground is one of twelve, positioned alongside the line at regular intervals, in January 1986, between Wolverhampton and New Street. They are the work of local sculptor Kevin Atherton. The idea was to give a little added interest to the route. The work was sponsored by West Midlands Arts, and British Rail made a contribution of £25,000. *(Stephen Widdowson)*

CHAPTER TWO : REAWAKENINGS, 1978-1986

[Diary : Notes : Cross City Leads The Way : The Rise of the Clock Face Time-Table : Freight]

Diary

1978

May 5th – Cross City service begins.

1979

May 14th – Through Euston-West Midlands-Shrewsbury trains increased from one to three daily.

October 1st – Experimental service provided five extra trains at Bromsgrove and Barnt Green.

1980

May 12th – Official closure date of Windsor Street Goods Depot, Aston.

1981

July 13th-August 7th – New Class 140 dmu works on the North Warwickshire Line.

November 2nd – One train each way on North East/South West route given over to HST operation.

December 12th – Official closure date of Swan Village coal depot.

1982

October 4th – Full HST service begins on NE/SW route through Birmingham.

1983

March 19th – Walsall-Lichfield line closes as a through route.

May 16th – Greatly improved service on the Stourbridge Line begins.

June 12th – Completion of the park and ride interchange at Cradley Heath.

1984

May 16th – Oldbury rebuilt as an InterCity station and renamed 'Sandwell & Dudley'.

August 7th – Maglev opens to the public, linking Birmingham International station and airport.

December 7th – Closure notice published for the southern section of the North Warwickshire Line.

1985

May 13th – Widney Manor now served by all local trains on the Leamington line.

June 21st – Another Millennium. At a ceremony at Wolverhampton station, Councillor George Howells names electric loco 86 433 (later 86 633) "Wulfruna" in recognition of the town's one thousand years of existence, although Wulfruna herself, King Edgar's sister, had no known connection with the place named after her until 994.

1986

January – Twelve black metal horses are positioned at intervals along the Birmingham-Wolverhampton line. They are the work of local sculptor Kevin Atherton and are seen as adding visual interest to the route.

January 20th – Sprinters begin to appear, chiefly on trains between New Street and Nottingham.

February 22nd-March 3rd – Reconstruction at Proof House, as bridges are replaced. Cross City North and Walsall services terminate at Duddeston, with bus connections to the city. Cross City North handled by Class 120 Swindon Cross Country dmus for the duration.

September 26th – Dudley Freightliner terminal closed.

Notes

Birmingham New Street had become established as the hub of the InterCity network in 1972. New services continued to develop. Direct trains between Manchester, Woverhampton, Birmingham and Brighton began in May 1979, with two daily workings in each direction. They ran via Reading and were normally hauled by a Class 47. The first southbound train left New Street at 01.33 in an attempt to tap a growing market, as a Gatwick Airport arrival at 05.01 was very convenient for early flights. Unfortunately the Brighton service was not very well publicised. Its strong selling point - a direct link between the West Midlands, Gatwick and the Brighton line without the hassle of crossing London - was not marketed in any serious way. In May 1986 the trains were diverted via Kensington Olympia, specially refurbished as a mini-InterCity station. The 1978 journey to Brighton, via Reading, took around four hours; in 1986 the two southbound trains took 3 hours 22 minutes. The 1999 time-table still offers just two trains each way, the fastest needing a minute under four hours, a sad reflection on the development or otherwise of this route's potential.

By 1980 there was a daily through train to Aberdeen via Edinburgh, with a Glasgow portion detached at Carstairs. The journey took 7hrs40m northbound, 17 minutes longer southbound. Today's Plymouth-Aberdeen 'Devon Scot' takes 7hrs6m from New Street, with its diesel High Speed Train running for 296 miles under the wires to Edinburgh - not necessarily progress.

High Speed Trains (HSTs) were phased in on the NE/SW route from autumn 1981, with just one train in each direction, running to existing timings. They took full charge of an accelerated daytime service the following May. There was virtually no spare capacity, as plans to invest in 18 train sets for this route had been pruned to 14 by HM Treasury, 13 to run the service plus a spare. No 125mph running was possible in the West Midlands, nor indeed anywhere between Penzance and Sheffield. Only on reaching the East Coast Main Line could the HSTs achieve their top speed. Superior acceleration helped shave time from the schedules. Typical examples from the 1982 time-table (1980 figures in brackets) were Birmingham to Sheffield 1hr26min (1hr35), to Newcastle 3hrs30 (4hrs) and to Bristol 1hr35 (1hr55).

In 1984 the local station at Oldbury had been rebuilt and upgraded, to emerge as the InterCity station of Sandwell and Dudley. It has a large car park and is within easy reach of M5 junctions 1 and 2. The station is served by all the Wolverhampton-Coventry locals, as well as most of the Wolverhampton-Euston trains. Unfortunately it is named after two places which it does not serve. There is no such place as Sandwell. The station remains in Oldbury, certainly not Dudley, three miles to the west. West Bromwich, the home of Sandwell Metropolitan Borough Council, is barely a mile away, so West Bromwich Parkway would be a more appropriate name. Sandwell and Dudley councils each contributed £30,000 towards the £1.3m cost of upgrading the station, so their generosity had to be marked somehow.

A popular television commercial of this era, promoting travel by High Speed Train, carried the slogan "This is the age of the train". All over the country, the train – the 1950s diesel multiple unit – was showing its age only too well. Replacements were urgently needed. In 1979 British Rail began canvassing PTEs with publicity material which featured its proposed lightweight dmu, later designated Class 140. The two-car unit weighed 38 tonnes and had 102 seats, with crush load space for 126 standing passengers. Fuel consumption was to be an economical 3.85 miles to the gallon. Despite their length of 20 metres, each car rode on just four wheels. This prototype first saw public service on the North Warwickshire Line between 13th July and 7th August 1981. The 'designers' (this is hardly an appropriate word) made no attempt to disguise its very basic appearance. It looked like a biscuit tin and the four little wheels meant that it rode like one. The press launch had taken place in Leeds on 4th June and the Directors General of all seven PTEs were in attendance to experience a journey to Ilkley. Afterwards, the DG of West Yorkshire PTE announced that he had informed BR that his PTE was interested in buying a fleet of such trains, about 50 in all. Mercifully, the WMPTE Director General did not follow suit which is why today, although many local services in the West Yorkshire area are in the hands of Class 141 production units, these wretched trains have never ventured into the West Midlands. Another vehicle for the PTEs to consider was the prototype Class 210 dmu, which proved to be over engineered and expensive. Instead of offering unnecessary luxury, or a cheap four-wheeled vehicle a century after production of four-wheeled carriages had ceased, the designers should have applied their minds to a natural successor to the traditional dmu. Eventually they did.

Four three-car prototypes were built in 1984-5, two by British Rail Engineering Ltd. (Class 150) and two by Metro-Cammell (Class 151). The Class 151 units underwent tests in February 1985, running in public service later in the year. Their distinctive appearance was caused by the roof mounted heater units. This was a very rare difficult moment for Birmingham's premier train builder. At the Washwood Heath plant, the shedding of 300 jobs due to lack of orders had left barely 40 manual workers on the payroll, the absolute minimum for keeping the factory open. Failure to secure an order for production 151s would threaten the works with closure.

Meanwhile, BREL had begun trial running its two Class 150s in June 1984, securing the order for the first production units. The government authorised expenditure on a further 120 units early in 1985. BREL, Metro-Cammell and Leyland all submitted tenders. On 5th November British Rail placed the order for 85 two-car units – with BREL. However, all was not lost for Metro-Cammell, which had won a £30m order for 25 emus for the Kowloon-Canton Railway less than two months earlier. BR was already looking beyond the Class 150 to a longer distance dmu and – also on November 5th – it was able to award Metro-Cammell the contract for 114 two-car 23metre units, which would be known as Class 156 Super Sprinters.

According to 'Modern Railways', the Class 150s were first dubbed 'Sprinters' by Alan Tame, Marketing Manager of BR Provincial, on 19th November 1984. The name is apt, as this generation of dmus has vastly improved acceleration and higher cruising speeds than the 1950s fleets. Some Sprinters began operating between Birmingham and East Anglia in January 1986. Time-table improvements in May that year provided an all-Sprinter two-hourly link between Birmingham, Derby, Nottingham and Lincoln, where Birmingham-Nottingham trains had scarcely existed previously. There was also an hourly service between Birmingham and Leicester, Sprinters alternating with the loco-hauled Norwich trains. All Shrewsbury-Aberystwyth trains were converted to Sprinter operation in a blaze of publicity at this time, arresting and reversing years of slow decline on the Cambrian main line. The service was further improved and extended as new long distance stock became available, first with Class 156s and later with 158s, which now provide a through train from Birmingham, Wolverhampton and Shrewsbury to Aberystwyth every two hours. Today the total journey time for the seven daily trains is around 3 hours; in the pre-Sprinter 1985 time-table there were five trains from Shrewsbury and the journey time from Birmingham was around 4 hours.

The Class 150 Sprinters have proved to be solid dependable workhorses, familiar on all the non-electrified West Midlands routes, first in their Provincial grey and two-tone blue, through the Regional Railways' variation to the green livery of Centro. The first of the 35 Leyland Class 155 two-car Super Sprinters entered service in 1987 where, before a third car was added to some 150s, their greater number of seats (160) provided extra accommodation on the increasingly busy New Street-Stourbridge-Worcester service. They were the first Sprinters to incorporate plug doors. A stylised athlete 'under starters orders' was an eye catching logo. These longer units (23m per car) had more comfortable seating and were visually distinguished by the large number of windows, eleven on each side of the saloon, compared to five on a Class 150. Within a few years most were converted to single cars and designated Class 153, for use on remote or short branches, including Stourbridge Town. The Metro-Cammell Class 156 units began entering service in 1987, followed by the top of the range Class 158s in the early 90s, to complete the Sprinter series. All Sprinters are powered by Cummins engines; all have a top speed of 75mph (90mph for the 158s).

The Sprinters did not, of course, take over all West Midland services overnight. First generation heritage dmus were needed for some peak hour workings until the autumn of 1994. The Cross City Line, apart from a few instances of exceptional rostering, has always been a Sprinter-free zone, converting straight from heritage dmus to heritage emus, before the new Class 323s were given a clean bill of health ....

During the 1970s and 80s there was still a large number of excursions, as there was both the stock and the management will to organise them. On the London Midland Region they were marketed under the brand name 'Merrymaker'. Some excursions were offered in traditional dedicated trains, others consisted of bargain fare block allocations in time-tabled trains. As 'Modern Railways' explained in 'Merrymaking is a serious business' (July 1981), *"In the current season, 1,500 different trips, options or journey opportunities are on offer. Block bookings are allocated to Merrymaker passengers (probably bent on two or more excursions) on timetabled trains. The majority of such trips are booked well in advance, very few on the day previous to travel and, as far as can be judged, the rate of abstraction from full-fare travel is very small."*

For those wanting to have a day out without straying far, a West Midlands Daytripper was ideal, covering the PTE area with a little more besides, as far as Lichfield and Stratford, for example. During the summer of 1986 a go anywhere day ticket (after 09.30 on weekdays) was just £1.50 adult, 75p child. A family ticket, for two adults and up to four children, cost £2.75.

There were other opportunities for leisure travel by train, at least two of which were unrepeatable and are now largely forgotten. In 1979 there were various events, exhibitions, etc. in the Ironbridge area to mark the 200th anniversary of the construction of the world's first iron bridge there. A temporary wooden platform was erected at ' Telford Coalbrookdale', within walking distance of the bridge itself, and a direct train service provided from Wolverhampton between 27th May and 2nd September. As the Ironbridge branch was busy with merry-go-round trains for the power station during the week, the passenger service could only run on Sundays, four trains in each direction with a £1 return fare. Most local stations in the West Midlands were still closed on Sundays. However, in 1986, on the Sunday of the bank holiday weekend, August 24th, most were opened specially to take motor sport enthusiasts to see the 'Super Prix', a race round a city centre circuit which the city fathers vainly hoped would become an annual fixture.

The photographer's son stands alongside the Class 140 lightweight dmu at Birmingham Moor Street, 1981. *(Alan Searle)*

(courtesy of Bob Pearson)

In 1981 the London Midland Region undertook an infrastructure review of the West Coast Main Line. At this date it was still assumed that electrification would continue until most lines of any importance had been energised. Rather than tackling a few lines piecemeal, as has actually been the case, there would have been a rolling programme of electrification, undertaken by a permanent team of experienced engineers. That this was not allowed to happen is one of the biggest tragedies of twentieth century British railway history. Amongst many other things, the 1981 review recognised the problems caused when electric trains were diverted over non-electrified routes. Details were published in 'Modern Railways' in March 1982. They make frustrating reading today:–*"Further long term electrification proposals will be developed on their merits, but the extension of electrification on adjoining routes makes it necessary to study the effects of this wider policy. There is a number of non-electrified secondary routes within the present West Coast electrified area that are often used as diversionary routes. Because of low line speeds and the need to stop to attach/detach diesel locomotives the diversions add considerably to journey times. But as network electrification increases the number of available diesel locomotives for this type of work will diminish... To overcome this problem five routes are proposed for electrification as soon as possible. They would be low cost schemes. The lines are Crewe-Kidsgrove($8\frac{3}{4}$ miles); Walsall-Rugeley($15\frac{1}{2}$ miles); Nuneaton-Birmingham($20\frac{3}{4}$ miles); Coventry-Nuneaton($10\frac{1}{4}$ miles); Sandbach-Hartford (12miles).*

Two Class 151 three-car dmus were built by Metro-Cammell in 1985 as prototypes for the West Midlands, intended as the first of many to replace the ailing 'heritage' units. However, Class 150 Sprinters were ordered instead. The 151s spent some time in public service in the Birmingham area and one is seen here leaving New Street for Lincoln on 12th March 1988. The seating was in various configurations to test customer reactions. At the time of writing both 151s are in store at Derby, awaiting their fate.

(Stephen Widdowson)

Two InterCity workhorses of yesteryear. 47 082 and 47 144 have both arrived at New Street with northbound cross country expresses, Tuesday 3rd August 1982. The locos will retreat, to be replaced by electric traction. Nowadays, High Speed Trains have reduced journey times on this core route, but given the excessive number of miles run under the wires by these diesel trains, and given the absence of plans for future main line electrification, is this progress? *(David Pagett)*

Examples of good 1970s station buildings are rare in Britain. 86 321 enters Birmingham International with a Euston-Wolverhampton train on 14th May 1981. *(David Pagett)*

Rail Blue traction variety at the Wolverhampton end of Birmingham New Street, 15th July 1983. *(David Pagett)*

31 410 approaches Water Orton with a train from Norwich on 14th March 1981, past the signal box which replaced an earlier one demolished in an accident in the 1950s. *(David Pagett)*

A sturdy 1960s-built workhorse, the Type 4 Class 47, is still working hard at the end of the century, with some examples even being rebuilt as Type 5 Class 57s for heavy freight duties. This class was familiar ever since new on the NE-SW Cross Country route through Birmingham. On 16th May 1988, 47 150 heads south with the 07.44 Edinburgh/07.54 Glasgow - Poole "Wessex Scot". The location is Kenilworth Junction, where the direct line from Berkswell once came in through the blue brick arches on the left. *(Andrew Bell)*

A Tyseley based 'heritage' dmu in the twilight of its years on the North Warwickshire Line, near Danzey, with a Snow Hill-Stratford service on 16th April 1990. *(Andrew Bell)*

Rural surroundings just over a mile from New Street. A Class 116 unit passes the site of Somerset Road station with a southbound Cross City service, 14th July 1990, by which date preparatory works for electrification had begun. *(Malcolm Keeley)*

A study in yellows at Shirley, 12th May 1984, with units for Moor Street (with the pre-Centro 'WM' logo) and Stratford.
(Malcolm Keeley)

A full house and more at Moor Street's three platforms, 7th July 1981. The units are (l.to r.) M50063, M50854, M50113 and M50316.
(Malcolm Keeley)

37 180 takes the Lichfield line at Ryecroft with a northbound tanker train, 20th January 1978. *(Michael Mensing)*

Class 50 Co-Co diesel electric No.50 016 "Barham" approaches Hatton station, 27th January 1979. The train is on the return leg of a round trip. Having formed the 09.55 Paddington-Worcester Shrub Hill, it then became the 12.35 Worcester-New Street-Oxford-Paddington. *(Michael Mensing)*

BR Derby-built Class 116 set M50840 pauses at Widney Manor with a Leamington train during the Midlands' last hard winter of the century, 12th December 1981. Services at Widney Manor were peak hour only until May 1985 and the station remained unstaffed until January 1989. *(Malcolm Keeley)*

Blue liveried 31 545 leaves Walsall for the Sutton Park line with a Bescot-Washwood Heath working, 3rd March 1995. The council car park, built in 1970, spans the tracks leading from the station. *(Roger Shenton)*

25 259 with an eastbound train on the Sutton Park line, 3rd November 1975. The train has paused at Sutton Park to shunt a van into the sidings of what was then an important Royal Mail sorting office. These sidings have gone but the line remains an important freight artery, so much so that in 1999 Railtrack proposed that it should be electrified, along with the Birmingham-Nuneaton route.

(Michael Mensing)

A scene which exists only in the memory. 20 183, still with its original four character headcode panel, shunts in the yard at Norton Junction, north of Pelsall on the Walsall-Lichfield line, 11th November 1976. *(Michael Mensing)*

The General Secretary of the National Union of Railwaymen, Sidney Weighell, about to cut the first sod at the site of University station, 11th January 1976. This ceremony marked the beginning of works for the Cross City Line. *(courtesy of Birmingham Post & Mail)*

Cross City Leads The Way

Apart from the brief appearance of passenger trains on the Wombourne branch (1925-1932) Cross City was the first new train service in the West Midlands since the opening of the North Warwickshire Line seventy years earlier in 1908. It was not, of course, a new line as such, merely the inspired joining of two very different train services to create a fast and reliable transport link in a natural corridor across the city centre. Since 1955 services on the northern half of the route, between New Street and Lichfield, had been expanding steadily. Areas served by this line, north of Erdington, had a large army of commuters.

South of the city centre the train service on the Redditch line had been saved from closure in 1965, but at the same time was reduced to just three trains a day in each direction. This was of little use to one of Birmingham's biggest employers, Cadbury's of Bournville, despite being next to the station. It was of no use whatsoever to the British Leyland car factory at Longbridge, to Birmingham University and Queen Elizabeth Hospital, or to the booming office district at Five Ways. All were next to the railway; none had stations. (The hospital site, unlike most places in Birmingham, also suffered from poor bus links at that time.) The need for a Cross City Line, and for these new stations, had been recognised in the WMPTE Passenger Transport Development Plan of 1972. Work was inaugurated on 5th January 1976 by Sidney Weighell, General Secretary of the National Union of Railwaymen, when he turned the first sod at the site of University station. He said ('Birmingham Post, January 6th), *"Increased bus and train services and an integrated road and rail network are the way to plan Britain's transport. I hope this message from the West Midlands will be noted at the Environment Department. It is the sort of example we would find refreshing if it were being followed in other areas. It is most imaginative."*

The creation of the Cross City Line cost about £7.4m, of which £1.1m was spent at Tyseley, installing four new servicing sidings for the 21 extra dmu sets that would be needed. Tyseley's loco-hauled stock was transferred to Duddeston and Oxley to make further space. £6.3m was spent on track alterations, signalling and stations. At Longbridge a nine-car stabling siding was installed south of the junction with the former Halesowen branch. The freight lines, the outer tracks on the four track section between Longbridge and Kings Norton, were upgraded to passenger standard. Three new crossovers were laid within New Street station to aid flexibility of this service, and two stabling sidings were provided at Four Oaks. Additional signals created extra capacity between University and Proof House; other signals were re-spaced for the same reason in the areas controlled by the mechanical boxes at Erdington, Sutton Coldfield and Four Oaks.

A new station was built at Five Ways, on the same site as the original, which had closed in 1944. A new station at Longbridge remained incomplete for several weeks after the train service had begun. A third new station, the instant runaway success in terms of usage, was University, built on a sharp curve next to the road connecting the university campus with the Queen Elizabeth Hospital complex. Since opening, this has been one of the busiest local stations in the West Midlands. The work patterns of many people who use it ensure that it is almost as busy off-peak as during the rush hours. The island platform at Northfield was abandoned as new outer platforms and buildings came into use, a new station encasing the old. The outer platforms at Kings Norton were enhanced and a new ticket office provided on the Pershore Road South entrance. The decaying 1880s Midland Railway buildings at Selly Oak were replaced. All these stations are in the same distinctive house style. The temporary wooden platforms at Butlers Lane, dating from 1957, were extended to

Many people in the public eye have mastered the art of the fixed grin! The Cross City Line was formally opened by the Secretary of State for Transport, William Rogers, at a cermony at University on 8th May 1978. Afterwards he sold a ticket to the Chairman of British Rail, Peter Parker, watched by the resident railman. *(courtesy of Birmingham Post & Mail)*

take six-car trains. Car parking spaces - all free as part of WMPTE policy - were dramatically increased at Four Oaks to 200 (from 60), Sutton Coldfield 100 (17), Kings Norton 80 (0) and Northfield 106 (20). Bus bays were provided at some stations to ease the policy of integration between train and bus. Some bus services were re-routed slightly to serve the stations, as at Northfield, the focus of three routes. WMPTE bus and train fares were priced on distance and at the same level. The Travelcard, valid on both, cost £3.40 per week, £10 for four weeks in 1978.

The train service began on Monday 8th May 1978 and was an instant success. By July 22,000 people were using it every day, rising to 30,000 by the end of the year. There were four trains an hour between Longbridge and Four Oaks, with extras in the peaks, an unprecedented frequency for the West Midlands. There was also a half-hourly service on Sundays, the first Sunday service on any local line in the Birmingham area for over ten years. Cross City meant just that, as people living north of the city but studying at the university, or with a hospital appointment, or who worked in an office near Five Ways, or at Longbridge, etc. discovered that they could now negotiate the city centre with ease.

People living along the same line beyond Four Oaks and Longbridge also wanted to share the benefits of the new service. Their county councillors, called on by British Rail to financially support extra trains to Redditch or Lichfield, hesitated at first. Hereford & Worcester CC supported an experimental service of five extra trains to Barnt Green and Bromsgrove in 1979, four of which were extensions of existing services to Longbridge. Initial financial support was for a trial period of just six months. Encouraged by the modest success of this modest investment, they supported an hourly service to Redditch from May 1980. The county's longer term financial commitment was uncertain at first and British Rail did not feel able to feature these trains in the national time-table until May 1983! The Cross City service was gradually expanded during the decade. Half-hourly trains reached Blake Street in 1984 and Lichfield City in 1986. By 1988 trains were extended to Lichfield Trent Valley, where the High Level platforms re-opened. An experimental fifth off-peak train, running semi-fast, began in 1986, but it proved unworkable and was withdrawn in May 1989, at which date the time-table became half-hourly on the Redditch branch and between the two Lichfield stations, with four trains per hour on the rest of the line, a frequency which remains in force at the present time. Electrification had to wait until the 1990s..........

In 1956, using the Class 120 Swindon-built Cross Country dmus, British Railways began a semi-fast service on the Birmingham-Stourbridge-Worcester-Hereford-Cardiff route. Between Snow Hill and Worcester calling points were Smethwick West, Stourbridge Junction, Kidderminster and Droitwich. It was successful for a number of years, but the decline began after 1967, when it transferred from Snow Hill to New Street. There was no promotion and no new initiatives, it just withered slowly. After 1969 none of these trains ran through to Cardiff and in 1971 the service was withdrawn completely. No stations were closed, so there could be no objections. This left the Stourbridge line with an hourly all stations service between New Street and Kidderminster. There was no service outside the peaks between Kidderminster and Worcester. For most practical purposes, Kidderminster had become a branch line terminus. Here was a suitable case for treatment.

One of the many sinuous curves of the West Suburban Line, looking north as it passes through University station during construction, 29th November 1977. *(courtesy of Railtrack)*

Five Ways under construction, 7th September 1977. To the right is the trackbed of the line which once led to the Midland Railway's Central Goods station, with the Worcester Canal behind the wall. *(courtesy of Railtrack)*

An immaculate six car train of WR suburban dmu stock enters Five Ways with the 17.46 Longbridge-Four Oaks, 22nd June 1978. Less than two months after the start of the Cross City service 20,000 people were using the trains every day. Beyond the Longbridge-Four Oaks core, with four trains an hour, Lichfield still had an hourly service and Redditch continued to endure just three trains per day.

(Michael Mensing)

Longbridge station during the evening peak on its second day of operation, Tuesday 9th May 1978. The trains were busy, the northbound platform as yet unfinished and passengers alighting from southbound trains had a long walk because of the position of the points. Much of this platform faces a freight only line.

(Malcolm Keeley)

A damp day in depressing surroundings at Rowley Regis. Two Tyseley based Metro-Cammell dmus form the 14.35 from Worcester Shrub Hill to Birmingham New Street and Lichfield City, 19th October 1974. This 'cross-city' service was never marketed as such, it followed no natural travel corridors and was mainly for operational convenience. The Shell fuel terminal generated considerable rail borne traffic. The depot closed and this part of the site is now occupied by the station car park. In 1974 Rowley Regis, formerly known as 'Rowley Regis & Blackheath' had an hourly off-peak service to Birmingham New Street; now there are four trains per hour, all to Snow Hill, Moor Street and beyond. *(Michael Mensing)*

Within the WMPTE area, New Street-Stourbridge trains became half-hourly in May 1979. The Stourbridge Town shuttle increased in frequency to connect with all the new trains. In May 1983 the wider service was completely recast. Existing trains were supplemented with an hourly semi-fast working to Worcester and beyond, calling only at Cradley Heath, Stourbridge Junction, Kidderminster and Droitwich. They were marketed under the brand name "Express Link". The line opened on Sundays for the first time since 1967, with a two-hourly semi-fast service, which became hourly the following year. The weekday semi-fast trains became half-hourly in 1987, giving two trains an hour from Birmingham to Kidderminster, four an hour from Stourbridge. The service north of Stourbridge was almost as intense as on the Cross City Line, and the ailing Town Car, one of Tyseley's Class 122 bubble cars, had never had to work so hard. At this kind of frequency passengers could just turn up and go, without needing to consult the time-table for most journeys. There was a 25% increase in passengers on the Birmingham-Stourbridge-Worcester-Hereford route between May 1983 and November 1984.

The start of the improved service in 1983 coincided with the closure of Kidderminster goods yard. Part of the site was converted for use as the station car park and part was acquired by the Severn Valley Railway for their Kidderminster Town station. The WMPTE sponsored car park at Stourbridge Junction is largely on land formerly occupied by the goods avoiding lines. By 1983 there were spaces for 313 vehicles and it was virtually full on most weekdays. It has since expanded to occupy the whole of the available land; usage has increased in parallel. The decaying pile at Cradley Heath was rebuilt during 1983, not a moment too soon. The northbound platform had been located north of the level crossing; both platforms were now positioned to its south. As at Kidderminster, the former goods yard was put to good use, as a WMPTE sponsored bus station and 102 space car park. Within two years the car park was generally full by the end of the morning rush hour and the number of passengers using the station had increased from 3,000 to 4,000 per day. The prospect of bus privatisation at this time, with its emphasis on competition rather than integration, cast doubt on the provision of any further schemes similar to those at Cradley Heath.

Car parks in themselves are hardly inspiring places, but WMPTE recognised their importance, along with useful bus connections at stations, as part of an improved train service package. A new car park with 78 spaces opened at Blake Street in 1984, along with 100 spaces at Chester Road. Small car parks were provided at Coseley and Marston Green, with a bus interchange at the latter. Widney Manor, which had been an unstaffed halt with just a handful of peak hour trains for decades, was provided with a full service from May 1985 in response to nearby substantial housing development. The station was completely rebuilt during 1984-85, with the provision of a ticket office and waiting room. Large car parks were laid on land once occupied by tracks which had been removed when the route was 'dequadrified' in 1966.

Throughout the years covered by this chapter – apart from small dips in 1981-82 caused by ASLEF strikes and the general recession – the number of passengers on local services rose consistently. This was despite WMPTE having to abandon its cheap fares policy, which caused an average fare increase of 67% (!) on 7th March 1982. Between November 1984 and November 1985 there was an increase of 2 million passengers journeys in the WMPTE area (7.5% of the 26.7m total), with a 12% increase on the Walsall line and 20% on Cross City South.

Outside the WMPTE area, and against the general trend, one route was proposed for partial closure. The North Warwickshire Line had only been kept open since 1969 because of a High Court Injunction, granted on the Friday before the due date because of arrangements made for replacement bus services, which did not follow the correct legal procedure. In July 1984, British Rail made an application for the injunction to be lifted and this was granted. On December 7th a closure notice was published for the southern section of the line, between Henley-in-Arden and Bearley Junction. Birmingham-Stratford trains were to be re-routed via Solihull, there was to be a Birmingham-Henley branch service (which could not have survived south of Shirley for long) and Wootton Wawen was to close. British Rail claimed that the line was costly to run and the double track south of Henley was an expensive luxury which would allegedly cost £5m over the next ten years, although it was in better condition than most of the rest of the line. Costs were reckoned to be six times greater than income, although this was not reinforced with any convincing statistics. There were no fewer than 7,077 objections. The statutory enquiry opened in January 1987 and by October of that year it reported that severe hardship would be caused by closure. Four local authorities - Birmingham City Council, Warwickshire County Council, Solihull Metropolitan District Council and Stratford-upon-Avon District Council – offered financial support, whereupon British Rail withdrew its closure proposal and the train service continued.

The Rise of the Clock Face Time-Table

Virtually all local rail services in the West Midlands, as in most conurbations, operate to a regular interval time-table. It is an essential feature of their dependability. It was not always thus. Before 1954 all local services ran at haphazard and infrequent intervals; they were not well used. Steam push-pull trains began running hourly between New Street and Sutton Coldfield in 1954, increasing to half-hourly with diesels to Four Oaks in 1956. This was followed by the introduction of regular interval diesel services on some Snow Hill routes in 1957. A new era had dawned.

It will be clear that this section considerably overflows both ends of this chapter's time span, but significant improvements did take place between 1978 and 1986. Equally clear, it would be complex and tedious to catalogue each time-table change as it happened. Instead, I have outlined all the regular interval services at ten year intervals, from 1959 to 1999. I hope this gives an overview which is easy to scan. The dramatic improvements can readily be appreciated, despite a few casualties during the 1960s. Not every service ran exactly at regular intervals, but all those included here did so at least in spirit if not quite to the minute.

[All frequencies given are for off-peak weekday services. NS=New Street, SH=Snow Hill.]

1959

half-hourly : NS-Four Oaks, hourly on to Lichfield City
hourly : SH-Kidderminster-(Bewdley SO)
hourly : SH-Dudley
hourly : SH-Henley-in-Arden (infrequent irregular service on to Stratford)
hourly : Wellington-Wolverhampton LL-SH-Lapworth (irregular service on to Leamington)
hourly : Wolverhampton HL-Walsall, two-hourly on to Lichfield and Burton
hourly : NS-Redditch (1960-1964)

1969

half-hourly : NS-Four Oaks, hourly on to Lichfield City
half-hourly : NS-Walsall, one fast via Soho Loop, calling only at Bescot
hourly : NS-Kidderminster
hourly : Wolverhampton HL-NS-Coventry
hourly : Moor Street-Leamington Spa
hourly : Moor Street-Henley-in-Arden, two-hourly on to Stratford-upon-Avon

1979

Cross City – every 15 minutes : Longbridge-NS-Four Oaks, hourly on to Lichfield City
half-hourly : NS-Birmingham International, hourly on to Coventry
half-hourly : Moor Street - Shirley, hourly on to Henley, two-hourly on to Stratford
half-hourly : Moor Street - Dorridge, hourly on to Leamington Spa
hourly : New Street - Kidderminster
hourly : New Street - Walsall
hourly : New Street - Wolverhampton

1989

Cross City – half-hourly from Redditch, forming two of four trains per hour Longbridge-NS-Lichfield City, two of which went forward to Lichfield Trent Valley.
four per hour : NS-Stourbridge Junction, half-hourly on to Kidderminster and Worcester
half-hourly : NS-Walsall
hourly : Walsall-Hednesford (opened April 1989, connecting with NS-Walsall trains above)
half-hourly : Coventry-NS-Wolverhampton
half-hourly : SH-Shirley, hourly on to Stratford-upon-Avon
half-hourly : SH-Dorridge, hourly on to Leamington Spa
hourly : NS-Leicester
hourly : Coventry-Leicester-Nottingham

1999

Cross City – half-hourly from Redditch, forming two of four trains per hour Longbridge-NS-Lichfield City, two of which went forward to Lichfield Trent Valley
Snow Hill group – six trains per hour through Snow Hill in the following sequence:–
Worcester-Kidderminster-SH-Leamington : Stourbridge-SH-Stratford : SH-Dorridge : Stourbridge-SH-Shirley : Stourbridge-SH-Dorridge : SH-Shirley
hourly : (in conjunction with the Snow Hill trains) Worcester-Stourbridge-NS
four per hour : NS-Walsall (two calling only at Tame Bridge), hourly on to Rugeley and Stafford
half-hourly : Wolverhampton-NS-Coventry
half hourly : NS-Leicester
hourly : Coventry-Leicester-Nottingham
hourly : (as part of longer distance services) Worcester Shrub Hill-Bromsgrove-NS

Longer distance regular interval 'non-InterCity' services developed in recent years include –
two per hour : NS-Coventry-Northampton-Euston semi-fast
hourly : NS-Wolverhampton-Shrewsbury, going forward alternately to Chester and Aberystwyth
hourly : NS-Leicester-Peterborough-Cambridge-Stansted Airport
hourly : SH-Solihull-Leamington-Banbury-Marylebone semi-fast
hourly : NS-Wolverhampton-Stafford-Crewe-Liverpool

Remaining irregular services
Tamworth is the largest town within a 25 mile radius of Birmingham without a regular interval service.
The Wolverhampton-Shrewsbury stopping service is infrequent and mainly irregular.
The Wolverhampton-Walsall service, reopened in 1998, runs at approximately 40 minute intervals.

Most lines without a regular interval service withered and died. The Sutton Park line closed in 1965. A handful of commuters prepare to board as 44914 enters Sutton Park c.1960 with a Birmingham train. *(courtesy of Birmingham Post & Mail)*

The Lichfield line prospered after the regular interval diesel service was introduced in 1956, so much so that the dmus needed heavy duty help during the peaks. D298 is seen at Erdington with a northbound local , April 1966. *(C.C. Thornburn)*

When slam door stock was the norm, long trains could call at short platforms; the onus was on the passenger to make sure the platform was there before he/she opened the door and stepped out. With modern stock the onus is on the guard, who controls all the doors, to make sure that the whole train is alongside the platform. Here a three-car Metro Cammell dmu calls at the two-car length platform at The Lakes with a train for Birmingham Moor Street at the start of an unforgettable summer, 1st June 1976. Trains ran to Stratford every two hours at this time. *(Peter Shoesmith)*

During the 1980s there were several arson attacks on the ex-LNWR timber framed station buildings on the Cross City Line. This is the scene at Wylde Green after one such attack on 24th August 1984. *(courtesy of Birmingham Post & Mail)*

Two-car Sprinter 150111 approaches Smethwick Rolfe Street with a train from Aberystwyth, 26th May 1987. *(Terry Walsh)*

Before the advent of the Class 321 emus, the New Street-Euston semi-fasts via Northampton, the 'little Londons' were worked by Class 317s. Unit 317 311 stands at Coventry bound for Euston on 12th July 1988. This service has prospered, later worked by eight-car 321s when they ran hourly. Most workings are now four-car again, but the frequency has been doubled to half-hourly. *(Terry Walsh)*

The Class 58 Type 5 heavy freight Co-Co locos were built 1983-87 by BREL at Doncaster. The fifty locos of this class are all fitted with 3300hp Ruston Paxman engines. 58 044 was named "Oxcroft Opencast" at a ceremony in Sheffield. (Oxcroft itself is in Derbyshire, near Bolsover, on the welter of freight only lines that cover the East Midlands coalfield.) The loco is running round its loaded MGR train, destined for Rugeley Power Station, at Rugeley TV, having arrived from the East Midlands via Wichnor Junction and the High Level-Trent Valley link at Lichfield, 27th May 1992. *(Roger Shenton)*

Freight

If the Class 66 is the freight loco of the 1990s, the Class 58 is its 1980s equivalent. These fifty machines were built by BREL at Doncaster between 1982 and 1987. They have a Co-Co wheel arrangement (6-wheeled bogies) and weigh 130 tonnes. They can haul very heavy trains in pairs or even in threes, with just one crew. All are equipped with slow speed control for use during merry-go-round (mgr) working, when the whole train crawls through a facility (eg; at a power station) at half a mile an hour, without stopping, while the wagons are loaded or discharged.

In design and appearance the 58s break with the past. Their immediate predecessor, the Class 56, was a 1970s development of the Class 47, first built in 1963. The 58s were intended to be simple to build and easy to maintain. Above the bogies is the steel underframe, 19.13 metres long, onto which the rest of the machine is mounted. The locomotive is of modular construction, with just six body sections bolted onto the underframe. None of them is load bearing, as that role is fulfilled exclusively by the underframe itself. Its strength is such that a crane can lift the loco by the underframe alone, at its central lifting points, without any distortion occurring. Because of the modular construction any one of the six body sections – such as a complete cab – can be replaced by another 'from stock' if necessary. The cab ends are wider than the body sides, giving the 58 its distinctive profile. Another obvious feature shows that the designers cared for the wellbeing of the fitters and maintenance men; there are no fewer than nine full height doors forming a curtain on each side of the body to allow ease of access to the engine room and equipment compartments, a feature that would have been welcomed on the Class 56, where such access is very limited. (For an interesting and comprehensive description of the Class 58, see 'Modern Railways', March 1983).

Rail freight was experiencing mixed fortunes at this time, although the general trend was down. It was a case of one step forward and two steps back. Some activities had outlived their usefulness, others were merely casualties of the general decline. Windsor Street Goods in Aston, with a capacity of 800 wagons, finally closed in 1980, despite having been electrified along with the main line in 1967. It had also served Birmingham's main gas works, but the steep decline in wagonload traffic and conversion to North Sea gas was a double blow that sealed its fate. Much of the former Great Western main line between Snow Hill and Wolverhampton remained open to freight after 1972 but it continued to fragment as small closures nibbled away at what was left. The spread of smokeless fuel brought about the closure of Swan Village coal depot in 1981, and with it the connecting link from Wednesbury Central. In the other direction, the link from Wednesbury to Wolverhampton Steel Terminal closed in 1983, although Wednesbury-Bilston lingered into the 90s to serve the Norton Barrow scrapyard. Dudley Freightliner Terminal had a precarious existence as traffic levels failed to live up to expectations. It had been scheduled for closure in 1981, when Freightliner generally was operating at a loss, but, *"with the development of new business in the West Midlands a joint management/staff committee has determined a way of retaining a 'small but viable' operation at Dudley"* ('Modern Railways' January 1982). The terminal eventually closed in September 1986.

Along with the general decline there were some improvements, although not all were long term. The Oldbury branch from Langley Green served the Albright & Wilson plant, which received chemicals by rail, chiefly chlorine, amounting to 24,000 tonnes in 1979. During 1980, 950 metres of sidings at the

Seen from the Market Street bridge, the distinctive shape of 58 004 approaches Hednesford with a southbound Sunday engineering train, 19th February 1989. *(John Whitehouse)*

47 060 approaches Wednesbury in May 1986 with the 4S88 Dudley-Glasgow Freightliner. Notice the track to the steel terminal, Ocker Hill Power Station and the abstract art caused by the pylons. Closure of Dudley Freightliner Depot did not help the Stourbridge-Dudley-Walsall line's viability. *(John Whitehouse)*

Although the Birmingham Snow Hill-Wolverhampton Low Level line closed to passengers in 1972, various fragments survived for freight. One section which clung to life by its fingertips was a single track beyond Wednesbury Steel Terminal, finishing at the Norton Barrow scrapyard, Bilston. Trains were trip worked as required by an 08 shunter from Wednesbury. On 15th May 1991, 08 428, having shunted the scrap merchant's yard, prepares to propel seven well-filled wagons back to Wednesbury. *(John Whitehouse)*

works were replaced and the new track set in concrete flush with the whole works' road area. This cost £250,000. In little more than a decade the branch fell into disuse. One of the West Midlands' more remote lines is the Pensnett branch, which leaves the OWW route at Kingswinford Junction. Little used for years, there were high hopes when LCP Properties and the French shipping company Jules Roy jointly opened a rail distribution warehouse at Pensnett on 5th June 1986. Perrier Water arrived in French wagons for onward distribution by road. Other incoming traffic was to include French wine, Swiss chipboard and zinc from Belgium. At the time of writing this branch line with international pretensions sees only occasional traffic.

Section 8 of the 1974 Railway Act enabled grants from government funds to be made to assist with the improvement of existing freight installations, or the provision of completely new ones. Half the cost of the 1980 improvements at Albright & Wilson was met by a Section 8 Grant. In the same way, application was made for a grant to construct a rail reception depot for finished steel at Round Oak. Long distance support was given by Poole Council, Dorset, as Poole docks handled over 50,000 tonnes of steel from the West Midlands, all of it arriving by road. The application was successful, and a grant of £1.15m was announced on 24th March 1984.

One strategically important freight link opened in 1983 was the 350-metre Oxley Chord, providing a direct connection between the Stafford and Shrewsbury lines at Wolverhampton. Southbound trains on either line could round the new curve and head north on the other. This was especially useful for merry-go-round workings between the Staffordshire coalfield and Ironbridge Power Station.

Today the Langley Green-Oldbury branch lies derelict. Formerly, it served the Albright & Wilson plant. A daily trip from Bescot delivered chlorine, often as part of a working which also served Handsworth cement works. The cement tanks were stabled in Rood End sidings while the main train went to Oldbury. On 24th April 1986 25 265 takes the sharp curve on the Oldbury branch leading to the dedicated sidings next to the plant. *(John Whitehouse)*

Pensnett Rail Distribution Depot is at the end of a branch from Kingswinford Junction on the Dudley-Stourbridge-Walsall line. In its time it has been used to tranship a wide variety of goods and materials, ranging from coal to Perrier Water, although it has seen little activity in recent years. In busier times, 47 283 is engaging in a complex shunting of Cargo wagons and Continental vans, having arrived from Bescot with what was then a daily trip working, 12th April 1988. *(John Whitehouse)*

'Crompton' 45 022 heads the morning Bescot-Toton freight past Rushall Crossing on 9th March 1984, ten days before closure of the Walsall-Lichfield line. The automatic full barrier crossing gates were installed shortly before closure. The 'Peaks' were known as Cromptons to railwaymen on account of their Crompton Parkinson electrical equipment. The pupils are in no hurry to reach school.

(John Whitehouse)

Wagonload traffic, unfashionable since the Beeching era, was taking a long while to die. There was also the dawning realisation that Freightliner was not a complete answer. Begun in 1979, Speedlink developed during the 1980s as a national system for carrying freight swiftly, efficiently and to a regular time-table. By 1981 nine routes radiated from the West Midlands. As well as general traffic there were more specialised movements, such as 'Steelink', 1,000 tonne trains of finished and semi-finished steel, which began running from Scunthorpe to Wolverhampton in 1980. When Rover started production of its 200 series cars in 1984, Speedlink was awarded the contract to move components from Cowley to Longbridge in daily trains of fifteen high capacity 53-tonne vans. Speedlink was generally acknowledged to be successful and reliable but unfortunately, in the run-up to privatisation, the cash starved railway industry in general, and Speedlink in particular, needed investment as infrastructure required renewal. No government investment was forthcoming and, despite industry-wide pleas, Speedlink was allowed to starve. The whole network closed, as rail freight declined further, in 1992.

Freight services could be closed without so much as a by your leave. If a profitable traffic flow became unprofitable, even if experience suggested that this was a temporary downturn, the service, or even a whole line, could be closed. BR was given a strict (and unrealistic) remit by HM Government to operate all freight at a profit at all times. Unlike non-profitable passenger services, there was to be no consideration as to whether a freight line or service formed a strategic part of the network, whether it was socially useful or whether it was better than the alternative of an increased number of lorry movements. No customer had the right of appeal against closure; there was no equivalent of the TUCC or the 'hardship' criteria. One victim of this strategy was the Walsall-Lichfield line, which closed as a through route in March 1984, leaving a four mile gap between Ryecroft Junction and Charrington's oil depot at Brownhills. The gap on the map soon became a gap in reality as the track was lifted during 1986. Lichfield-Brownhills was singled and a 20mph limit imposed. A glance at the map will show the importance of this line, a direct and easily graded route between Bescot and the whole of eastern England from Derby northwards. One item in 'Modern Railways' (February 1984) summarised the hopelessness of the situation in terms of both freight and passenger traffic –

"In December, West Midlands and Staffordshire County Councils made a joint appeal to British Rail to request the early completion of a feasibility study into the reopening of the Cannock-Rugeley line. The two County Councils also requested that BR should delay implementation of its proposal to close the freight only Walsall-Lichfield line at the turn of the year to allow consultations to take place about the route's potential as a passenger railway."

Passenger trains reached Cannock again in 1989, but the Walsall-Lichfield line was ignored. Worse was to follow.

CHAPTER THREE : STEAM REVIVAL

[Birmingham Railway Museum : The Severn Valley Railway : Along the Main Line]

The Birmingham Railway Museum during a "King & Castle" Gala Day. Castles 5080 "Defiant" and 7029 "Clun Castle" frame the unmistakable bulk of 6024 "King Edward I". *(Robert Jones)*

Birmingham Railway Museum

Birmingham Railway Museum is based at Tyseley, the home of a former Great Western double roundhouse engine shed which opened in 1908 with an allocation of 70 locomotives. It closed in 1967 and was largely demolished in 1969. During 1968 the former coaling stage was converted into a shed for preserved locos and on June 6th that year a ceremony was held there to mark the restoration of ex-LMS "Jubilee" No.5593 "Kolhapur". At first, the museum was open only by appointment, but regular hours became the norm after the first Open Day on 13th September 1970. Since that time the museum, now a registered educational charity, has steadily expanded. It offers an interesting family day out and a reminder of our railway history. But there's much more to it than that.

In the early days the museum, like most railway preservation societies, had barely sufficient human and financial resources to cope, as large numbers of steam locomotives were withdrawn from service with indecent haste. The members at Tyseley, mainly committed and hard working amateurs with a limited budget, could only react to the best of their ability, salvaging what they could as events quickly unfolded. With over thirty years experience, today's museum does not just react; it anticipates circumstances and initiates change. This proactive policy is the key to its present success. Consider the age of the volunteers themselves......

Those men who did the pioneering work during the 1960s and 70s almost invariably acquired their interest in railways during childhood. The lure of steam is a mystery even for many of those drawn to it, but the steam locomotive is the machine, more than anything else made by man, that seems almost to come alive, with a breath and personality all its own. As the original members grow older and fewer, Birmingham Railway Museum, like all railway preservation societies, will need an influx of new blood in order to continue.

Many younger people, brought up with computer technology, see railways as old fashioned and 'uncool', often viewing those who are interested in them as rather odd. Given the right circumstances, this perception can change. There will always be some young people in every generation who have a passion for machinery and a wish to get their hands dirty – ask the owner of any motorbike.

Bob Meanley is chief engineer at Tyseley Locomotive Works, a constituent part of Birmingham Railway Museum. Over the years there have been various locos languishing on site as they await restoration. By 1995, 4983 "Albert Hall", the tenth such machine to be rescued, had been parked at the shed's surviving turntable, exposed to the elements, for 25 years! Early that year, the difficult job of restoration began. (It was described in "Railway Magazine", March 1999). Bob's son, Alastair, had

shown an interest in railways as a small boy. On a visit to Tyseley aged ten, he and a friend were so keen that - under strict supervision - his father even let him do minor work expanding the boiler tubes of a pannier tank. Some six years later Alastair and his friend, Dean Morris, carried out preliminary overhaul work on the firebox of pannier tank No.7760, and on the boiler of 9600. By now they formed the nucleus of a group of like minded lads, all eager for the challenge that "Albert Hall" had to offer. The 'Tyseley Seven' swung into action.

The overhaul of this locomotive, at a time when most of the lads were still in full time education, involved almost three years' work, an estimated total of 11,000 man hours. They were supervised, mainly by Bob, but were essentially responsible for most of the main aspects of the restoration – cleaning the motion, making new bushes, the overhaul of cylinders, pistons and connecting rods, not to mention most of the painting and the little task of re-tubing the boiler. The quality of the workmanship, passed by former BR boiler inspector Sam Foster, was never inany doubt. The only surprise was the identity of the loco. During overhaul, it was discovered that many parts were stamped with the number 4965, that for "Rood Ashton Hall". The frames were found to be of a type fitted only to the first eighty Halls, so could not have been fitted new to 4983. As the frames are the core of a steam locomotive it was decided that this hybrid, seemingly a victim of cross-cannibalisation in the dying days of steam, was essentially "Rood Ashton" rather than "Albert".

David Fisher, one of the volunteers, baptised the buffer beam with champagne on completion on 4th May 1998 (see left). Following a satisfactory inspection in September 1998, Rood Ashton Hall had its first public outing by working the "Shakespeare Express" on 20th December. The skills of the Tyseley Seven were recognised the following month when they won the Heritage Railway Association's Small Groups Award. At the time of writing, two members of the seven, Alastair Meanley and Nick Davies, work full time at the loco works and the other five continue to serve as volunteers, surely an encouraging sign for the future.

There are currently fifteen locomotives at the museum, many in working order. The works undertakes heavy overhauls and can provide new main parts, both for its own stock and other railways. Recent contract work has included new frames for the A1 Pacific "Tornado", and provision of a new boiler for K1, the world's first Garrett loco, brought back from Tasmania to run on the reopened 2' gauge Welsh Highland Railway. Tyseley also fulfils a contract with Fragonset Railways on today's main line, maintaining six Class 47s which operate some of the Virgin Cross Country trains.

One of the most difficult and unusual challenges for any railway organisation today is to build a new steam locomotive from scratch. Successful replicas have been built, notably a "Locomotion" and a "Rocket", which took part in the railway cavalcade marking the 150th anniversary of the Stockton & Darlington Railway in 1975. Tyseley has attempted a working replica of its own, a copy of a 'Bloomer'. In 1850 Mrs.Amelia Bloomer, an American feminist, publicised new loose-fitting trousers, named after her, as a way of liberating women from the ankle length dresses of the day. The fashion soon crossed the Atlantic and the following year James Edward McConnell, Locomotive Superintendent of the LNWR, produced a new 2-2-2 type of express engine, nicknamed the 'Bloomer'. "The History of the London and North-Western Railway", published in 1914, pompously distanced itself from the truth when commenting – *"What ill-chance saddled these engines with such an uneuphonious name it is hard to say, seeing that none of them was ever named 'Bloomer'."* Tyseley's Bloomer, a brave attempt, remains incomplete due to lack of funds.

One of the most familiar shapes to devotees of anything Great Western is that of the pannier tank, a type once numbered in hundreds. These were humble workhorses, not glamour machines, and few escaped the cutter's torch. Three that did are in Tyseley's collection – 7752 and 7760 of the 5700 Class (49 tons, a Collett design of 1929) and 9600, built in 1945 to a Hawksworth modified design with a larger cab. 7752 ran between Tyseley and Stratford in 1974, after which there were no public appearances on a main line by any pannier tank until 1999. After several years in store, 9600 was restored to working order

Years of hard graft will be necessary before this loco moves under its own steam again. This was 5080 "Defiant", newly arrived at Tyseley from Barry scrapyard in 1980. *(Robert Jones)*

Looking superb after restoration, 5080 "Defiant" at Tyseley's 1990 Gala Day. *(Robert Jones)*

BRM poster of 1987 *(Robert Pearson collection)*

Alastair Meanley, one of the 'Tyseley Seven', busy inside the boiler during restoration work to "Albert Hall", although it proved to be the boiler of 4983 "Rood Ashton Hall", 16th January 1998. *(Robert Jones)*

at Tyseley during 1996 and, on 29th April 1999, hauled a special from Shirley to Stratford and back. The museum also plans to secure certification for main line running for 7760, so that two panniers can double head excursion trains, an impressive spectacle indeed!

Birmingham Railway Museum does not own any track outside the Tyseley site, yet its trains are increasingly familiar on the main line. For several years there have been specials to Stratford-upon-Avon on certain summer Sundays, the "Shakespeare Express". During 1999 these trains, usually hauled by "Rood Ashton Hall", ran on June 20th, then weekly between 11th July and 5th September, and on five more Sundays before Christmas. The service consisted of two round trips between Birmingham Snow Hill and Stratford, and included a stop at Tyseley. The "Shakespeare Express" was promoted as 'England's Fastest Regular Steam Train', attaining a speed of 60mph. This is an ideal way to enjoy the scenic delights of the North Warwickshire Line and to experience the loco working hard as it pulls up the continuous nine mile grade from Wootton Wawen to the summit at Earlswood.

Birmingham is the only place in Britain with anything like a regular steam service into the city centre and this could provide an excellent marketing opportunity. The old Moor Street terminus is decaying but still intact, with most of the track in situ. Restoration would present a number of interesting possibilities, making it an ideal terminus for the "Shakespeare Express" and other excursions. The platforms could be refurbished, with replica 'original' lighting and period advertisment hoardings. Much of the former ticket and administrative area, fronting the concourse and the street could be converted into a hands on visitor centre and exhibition area. One of the platforms could perhaps be semi-permanently occupied by a period train, as has happened successfully at Windsor. The refurbishment of the old Moor Street would attract visitors and help the regeneration of this part of the city, sandwiched between the Bull Ring and the area of Digbeth centred on Millenium Point. The development of Moor Street would certainly raise the profile of the Birmingham Railway Museum and its trains, helping its long term future at a time when some members of the rising generation appear to be offering it a long term commitment. If Moor Street terminus is not to become a railway station again, its prime position makes it certain that sooner, rather than later, it will be swept away and the site redeveloped to the exclusion of the railway.

Severn Valley Reflections. Black Five No.45000 pauses at Highley with a mid-week empty stock working, waiting for the road following a passenger train. Vic Smith was the driver. c.1982. *(David Postle)*

The Severn Valley Railway

The SVR runs for sixteen miles, linking Kidderminster, Bewdley and Bridgnorth. The line opened in 1862 and closed in 1963. Strenuous efforts were made to save it and the Severn Valley Railway Company was formed in 1965. It re-opened in stages, firstly between Bridgnorth and Hampton Loade, which saw its first public passenger train on 23rd May 1970. Services were extended to Bewdley in 1974 and Kidderminster Town in 1984. Behind these few bland sentences lie thousands of hours of hard voluntary work to turn a semi-derelict branch line into a thriving railway and a major tourist attraction. The SVR is now one of the busiest and most important preserved lines in Britain, with five engines in steam at the height of the season. Stock includes about 28 locomotives - the figure fluctuates as some are owned by individuals and on loan to the railway - with more than 60 passenger coaches and 70 freight vehicles, some awaiting restoration. There is an extensive engineering workshop at Bridgnorth. The railway's Victorian stations at Bewdley, Arley, Highley, Hampton Loade and Bridgnorth, have all been beautifully restored.

The Severn Valley Railway has a permanent staff of 70, headed by the General Manager, Alun Rees. With its headquarters in Bewdley, it is the largest employer in the town. There is a volunteer staff of more than 1,100. Some turn up on a casual basis, perhaps twice a year, to offer any general help. Others spend most weekends on the line. Volunteer labour is not necessarily casual, as all the key jobs – engine crew, guards, signalmen, booking clerks – obviously have to be rostered. Most volunteers are male, but there is an appreciable number of ladies, *"who bring their own brand of enthusiasm and, to a degree, a civilising influence"*, said Alun. The women work as shop assistants, signallers, guards. Four are firemen (perhaps that should read firewomen or firers?) who will be promoted to drivers. *"They are aware that they are trying to invade a male world, so they try harder and feel they have to be that much better in order to get accepted."*

There is a thriving Junior Club, open to anyone aged between 9 and 14. From the age of 14 club members can work on the railway, always under supervision on a one-to-one basis, probably in the signalboxes or the depot. At 16 they become full members of the volunteer staff and can work on the railway in their own right. The influence of the rising generation was seen to good effect on March 13th 1999, when the first SVR train crewed entirely by men born since the end of steam on British Rail in 1968 took to the rails. They were driver Jason Houlders (29), fireman Andrew Sweet (21) and guard John Price (19).

Another important age group is the 50 somethings, those who have taken early retirement but remain very active. They tend to devote a lot of time to the railway, which sees them as vital. *"Without their help we would have great difficulty in providing any kind of midweek services"*, said Alun. Although primarily a steam railway, the SVR is not trapped in the steam age. One volunteer is an IT expert, who writes programs for the railway's computers on weekdays, doubling as a driver at weekends.

It is perhaps only a slight exaggeration to say that the railway is the biggest single attraction in Kidderminster, Bewdley and Bridgnorth. A recent survey of guest houses and hotels undertaken by Wyre Forest District Council found that 80% of visitors had come to the area to visit the SVR. 1998 was the fourth consecutive year of growth, which saw a turnover of £3.193m. 212,500 passengers were carried in 1998, only slightly below the best ever figure of 213,000 for 1990, the 25th anniversary year.

As with most heritage railways, there are two main types of user – rail enthusiasts and day trippers. It may come as a surprise to learn, from SVR's own survey, that only 9% of users would describe themselves as 'enthusiasts'. Alun Rees spoke plainly, *"Our bread and butter is mum, dad and the kids and we neglect that fact at our peril. Neither this nor any other preserved line will ever make a living out of railway enthusiasts. If they are the only people you appeal to, you're destined to failure."*

Most visitors come from within a fifty mile radius and for many children, who almost always travel by car, part of the excitement is going on a train, not merely a steam train. However, *"The days when people came to ride on a heritage railway simply because it is there are long gone."* Therefore the line has to be offered as an important part of a larger package to broaden its appeal. Throughout the year there are special events aimed at a wide variety of people. Thomas the Tank Engine weekends are increasingly popular. The books come to life as suitably disguised engines manoeuvre in the station area at Kidderminster, directed by the Fat Controller over the PA system. There used to be one such weekend per year, rising to four by 1999. The 1940s weekend is another established part of the calendar, with vintage military vehicles on display, reduced admission for those able to produce a genuine wartime identity card and a Glenn Miller style big band concert on the platform on the Saturday night. There is a Classic Road Vehicle Day every October, with vintage buses providing an alternative to the train between Kidderminster and Bewdley. Every autumn sees a three day Steam Gala in September, followed by a Diesel Gala in October, *"and our biggest nightmare is thinking what to do on the gala weekends"*, confessed Alun, *"because if we keep repeating ourselves they will just die. The 1998 Steam Gala, for example, was built around the LNER. We have the biggest rake of teak-bodied Gresley coaches in working order in the country but no LNER loco. We hired one in and built the gala around that, selling the SVR as the only place where you could see LNER locomotive and stock together! It worked."*

Recently, the line has been successfully marketed to ramblers, promoting walks from SVR stations, the natural beauty of the area and the fact that Bridgnorth is an interesting town which can be reached by train. The line's latest station is popular with ramblers and picnickers. Country Park Halt opened in 1995 on the site of Alveley Colliery. Trains call only by request, but in fair weather and at weekends few go through without stopping.

The Santa Specials are, without question, the busiest trains of the year, every year. They began in 1974, probably earlier than on any other railway. Trains run from Kidderminster to Santa's Grotto at Arley and a gift for each child is included in the fare. In 1998 there were fourteen trains a day to Arley, with 98% loadings. 33,000 people were carried on the three weekends before Christmas. Advance booking is compulsory.

The biggest boost to traffic came with the extension of the service from Bewdley to the new station at Kidderminster Town. The station buildings are based on the 1890 design for Ross-on-Wye, Herefordshire. The track layout is different, as Ross was a through station but Kidderminster Town is a terminus with a single island platform. It opened in 1984. There is a large car park adjacent, with extra parking available nearby on busy weekends, because most people arrive by car. The main line station is alongside, with a half-hourly service and through ticketing to the SVR. A small percentage of SVR passengers arrive by main line train, but few take advantage of the through ticketing - only 473 did so during the whole of 1998.

The Severn Valley Railway is familiar to many people through film and television. Recent examples include "Howard's End" and the series "Oh, Dr.Beeching". The railway cannot physically expand any further, as there is no chance of relaying the line between Bewdley and Hartlebury, or north of Bridgnorth to Shrewsbury. There is a large carriage shed and repair shop at Kidderminster. The SVR is an asset to the communities along its route and it looks certain to have a bright future.

Within the Kidderminster station area is Kidderminster Railway Museum, housed in a GWR goods shed built in 1878 to handle wool for the carpet industry on the upper floor and grain for the adjacent flour mills on the ground floor. In later years it was adapted for use as a parcels office. It closed in the early 1980s, opening as a museum on the 1990 August Bank Holiday weekend. It lies alongside the SVR but is administered separately. It is a registered charity and owns some of the adjoining land, on which it plans to erect a GWR stable block, a weighbridge and an ex-Great Western signal box. There will be level crossing gates for display and a siding for the museum's pre-Grouping freight stock, some of which needs substantial restoration.

Inside there are displays of totems, nameplates and memorabilia, plus some more unusual items, such as a GWR Time Disc, a decoding device for converting clock time into telegraphic messages, as telegraph code used only letters. There is even a collection of assorted signal post finials forming a frieze near the ceiling. Nearby is an operational signal frame, retrieved from Rogart North on the Inverness-Thurso line. A typical Midland Railway booking office, using some items from the original Alvechurch station, forms a very attractive feature. The upper floor is used for film shows, conferences and exhibitions. Its library houses a large photographic collection, stored and catalogued on computer. If the museum develops as planned over the next few years it will be an increasingly valuable part of the railway site at Kidderminster.

4-6-0 No.7812 "Erlestoke Manor" about to leave Arley with a SVR Santa Special - plus the Old Gentleman himself – 19th December 1982. The fingerboard shows all departures terminating at Bewdley as the extension to Kidderminster was not yet operational.
(courtesy of Birmingham Post & Mail)

A goods train at Highley, pannier tank 5764 in charge, during the summer of 1979. First vehicle behind the loco is a Loriot L type well wagon, only seven of which were built by the GWR between 1926 and 1934. They were intended for transporting traction engines, bulldozers, caravans and the lorries of the day. The second vehicle, built by the GWR in 1899, was a special well wagon for carrying ready creosoted and chaired sleepers from the depot at Hayes. *(David Postle)*

Along the Main Line

After August 1968 steam was banned from British Rail for ever. For ever lasted until October 1971, when "King George V" was allowed onto the main line with the first of many steam specials. Although such trains are often a spectacular sight, it is easy for me to chose the most memorable. On 22nd November 1997 two Moguls attempted something never tried before. They would storm the Lickey Incline without stopping for a banker. Along with about three thousand others I took a vantage point near the Lickey. I was on rising ground, near Pike's Pool, from where much of the Incline was visible. Jaws dropped as the train raced through Bromsgrove at 60mph, storming the bank with an ever more dramatic display - a feast for the eyes and an amazing assault on the ears. The summit was cleared at about 12mph, the exhaust hung for several minutes in the clear still air and the onlookers remained silent, stunned by what they had just witnessed.

I have many memories of steam, mostly from childhood – locos on shed at Bescot, a 'King' entering Snow Hill with the 9am to Paddington, away on holiday behind the 'Atlantic Coast Express' – but if I could take only one steam memory to that mythical desert island, it would have to be the "Lickey Incliner".

In May 1992 GWR 4-4-0 No.3440 "City of Truro" passes Water Orton en route from Derby to Didcot with a railtour. City of Truro had a relatively short time in steam before being called back to the National Collection as a static exhibit. The buildings at Water Orton were destroyed by fire shortly afterwards and a 'bus shelter' is all that is provided on the platform now. The station had been well cared for by two rail women, who kept the waiting room spotless, also providing books for passengers to read and borrow, and jigsaws to do whilst waiting for a train. The remaining station buildings at road level, which had been threatened with demolition, are now listed. *(Michael Denholm)*

Two Moguls – ex-GWR 7325 and ex-LMS 2968 – make a truly spectacular sight as they attack the 1:37 up to Blackwell with the Pathfinder Tours "Lickey Incliner" on 22nd November 1997. It was estimated that up to 3,000 people gathered alongside the incline to witness the spectacle, with one man flying in specially for the day from Amsterdam. This brilliant photograph completely captures the atmosphere of a memorable occasion. *(Stephen Widdowson)*

During March 1990 King Class 4-6-0 No.6024 "King Edward I" approaches Small Heath with its first run on BR since restoration. It is hauling empty stock from Derby to Didcot on its test train. A now vanished Pressed Steel dmu heads towards Moor Street from Stratford-upon-Avon. Small Heath Bridge suffered bomb damage during the war, the replacement sides on the damaged section, partly hidden by steam, are lower and minus the curved top. The waste ground behind the King is now occupied by Small Heath Highway.

(Michael Denholm)

During April 1995 BR Standard Pacific No.70000 "Britannia" (the first BR Standard loco to enter service, in 1951) approaches the site of Bromford Bridge racecourse station with an InterCity private charter to Derby. The train is about to pass under Bromford Lane bridge. The sidings on the right have since been realigned to make way for the new Spine Road between the M6 and the railway.

(Michael Denholm)

46443 has just crossed Victoria Bridge with the 09.45 Kidderminster-Arley "Santa Special", 14th December 1997. *(Andrew Bell)*

46521 approaches Arley with the 09.45 "Santa Special" from Kidderminster, 29th November 1998. *(Andrew Bell)*

The first bodyshell for the Scotrail Class 334 Juniper emus. *(courtesy of Alstom)*

The business end of a Class 460 Gatwick Express, 'Darth Vader' unit. 31st March 1999. *(John Boynton)*

Metro-Cammell built North of London Eurostar set 3309/3310 passing Rugeley Trent Valley on a training run from Manchester to Bletchley, 9th March 1998. *(Roger Shenton)*

Coradia dmu 175 101 on static testing at Kidderminster SVR, 9th August 1999. *(Bob Sweet)*

Outer suburban improvement. The Birmingham-Walsall-Hednesford service was extended to Rugeley Town on 2nd June 1997. Class 150 Sprinter 150 011 leaves the Chase Line and approaches Rugeley Trent Valley – as empty stock and to cross over only – on the pre-service 'Fun Day', Sunday 1st June, Rugeley Power Station forming the backdrop. Further extension to Rugeley Trent Valley and Stafford followed twelve months later. *(Brian Moone)*

A Jewellery Line Class 150 Sprinter bound for Stratford passes a Midland Metro tram bound for Wolverhampton at The Hawthorns, 21st June 1999. *(John Boynton)*

A Cross City 323 heads north at Bournville, 22nd July 1999. *(John Boynton)*

323s for Coventry (left) and Wolverhampton cross at Berkswell, 1st July 1999. *(John Boynton)*

60 095 with an MGR train, probably from Mid-Cannock Opencast to Buildwas Power Station, approaches Walsall from Ryecroft Junction, 28th January 1997. *(Brian Moone)*

60 086, northbound at Kingswinford Junction, with train 6Z69, the 08.19 Boston-Round Oak steel coil train. This was the first day of the new service from Boston Docks, which re-opened to rail. The train runs twice weekly as required. Were the Stourbridge-Dudley-Walsall line to be restored as a through route this train would follow a more direct route and approach Round Oak from the north. *(Brian Moone)*

General Motors-built 66 031 enters the Sutton Park line at Ryecroft with a train of empty steel carriers from Wolverhampton Steel Terminal to Lackenby, Tees-side, 26th March 1999. *(Roger Shenton)*

EW&S liveried 60 020 with a MGR train for Rugeley Power Station about to pass under Albert Street bridge, Walsall, 11th August 1998. *(Roger Shenton)*

M40 Trains. A Class 165 Turbo alongside the motorway at Lowsonford, south of Lapworth, 25th July 1996. *(Andrew Bell)*

158 797, in the new Central Trains livery, on the Lickey Incline with the 09.00 Cardiff-Nottingham train, 21st June 1999. *(Bob Sweet)*

BEFORE & AFTER

'Before' at what was then "Acocks Green and South Yardley" as 5100 Class 2-6-2T No.4168 leaves with the 12.30pm from Snow Hill to Lapworth, 8th July 1961. 84E on the smokebox door indicates the loco's home shed, Tyseley. *(Michael Mensing)*

A Chiltern Railways Class 168 'Clubman' Turbo approaches Acocks Green with a Marylebone train, 5th September 1998. *(John Boynton)*

The footbridge at Bentley Heath Crossing, Dorridge, was a good vantage point from which to observe 'West Country' Bullied Pacific No.34052 racing south with a football special returning from Birmingham to Southampton, 27th April 1963. The 11-coach train may look an exhilarating sight but the mood of those in board would have been despondent. Southampton had just lost the FA Cup semi-final – played at Villa Park – to Manchester United, by the only goal. Southern Region daytime headcodes were white discs rather than oil lamps. *(John Edgington)*

A Class 168 'Clubman' Turbo of Chiltern Railways heads away from the camera with a Marylebone-Snow Hill train, 1st June 1999. The passage of 36 years has turned small conifers into giant weeds. *(John Boynton)*

This superb shot of the former Bloxwich station, looking north, shows a Metro Cammell dmu bound for Rugeley Trent Valley, plus the silhouette of an ex-LNWR 0-8-0 Super D. Note the distinctive station buildings, gas lamps and a lower quadrant LNWR home signal – 27th March 1964. The siding to the left of the platform exists today and is used by trip freights to Bloxwich Spelter Works and by engineering trains. *(Peter Shoesmith)*

Not really as rural and charming as it looks. The 1989 station at Bloxwich is a basic halt inconveniently sited away from the town centre, well screened from nearby housing and prone to vandalism. There are suggestions that it should be abandoned and replaced by a staffed station on the original site. Nevertheless, this is a most attractive photograph, as 150 129 leaves with a Stafford-New Street service on 16th April 1999. *(John Whitehouse)*

5917 "Westminster Hall" passes Kidderminster with an 'Old Worse & Worse' relief train, from Wolverhampton Low Level to Evesham, Whit Monday, 6th June 1960. *(Brian Moone)*

A Class 158 dmu approaches Kidderminster with the 09.47 Great Malvern-Birmingham New St, 27th May 1999. *(John Boynton)*

Spring Road on 22nd March 1957, as 2-6-2 tank No.5156 departs with the 10.02am from Stratford-upon-Avon to Birmingham Moor Street. Spring Road was a 'Platform', that curious hybrid unique to the Great Western, having neither the status of a fully appointed station nor the basic facilities of a halt. The buildings to the right of the train accommodated staff and a small parcels office.

(John Edgington)

The vegetation advances. Spring Road on 19th May 1999, as a Class 150 Sprinter departs for Stratford-upon-Avon. *(John Boynton)*

Widney Manor station on opening day, 1st July 1899. *(courtesy of Solihull Education, Libraries and Arts)*

Exactly one hundred years later, Turbo unit 168 002 hurries away from the camera at Widney Manor with the 10.30 Snow Hill-Marylebone service, 1st July 1999. *(John Boynton)*

CHAPTER FOUR : AN UNFINISHED JOURNEY, 1987-1999

[Diary : Notes : Passengers Once More : Freight : Made in Birmingham : Two Hours to London : Plans & Schemes]

Diary

1987

September 12th – Snow Hill Tunnel opened to the public.
September 26th – Last day Moor Street terminus open.
September 28th – New Moor Street station opened; service trains terminate here until October 5th.
October 5th – Public passenger services begin at the new Snow Hill station.

1988

May 14th – Bedworth station opened.
November 28th – Cross City service extended to Lichfield Trent Valley.

1989

January 17th – Widney Manor becomes a staffed station once more.
April 10th – Walsall-Hednesford re-opened.

1990

February 7th – Approval given for electrification of the Cross City Line.
May 11th – Last day for the early morning Walsall-Coventry (SX) direct train, the last regular passenger train over the Aston-Stechford line.
May 14th – New soutbound platform comes into use at Bromsgrove.
June 4th – Tame Bridge station opened.
October 2nd – Bloxwich North opened.
December 3rd – Provincial becomes Regional Railways.

1991

July 6th – Speedlink axed.

1992

February 11th – Announcement of a proposed InterCity station for Birmingham at Heartlands.
April 5th – Last day of the traditional regions of British Rail.
November 26th – First electric train in public service on the Cross City Line, 17.28 New St.-Blake St.

1993

February – New footbridge opened at Birmingham New Street, with an exit to Navigation Street.
March 19th – Last day Walsall-Dudley-Stourbridge line in use as a through freight route.
May 17th – Revival of through trains between Birmingham Snow Hill and London, after 26 years.
July 12th – Full electric service begins on the whole Cross City Line.
October 17th – First trial run of a Birmingham-built Eurostar set, No.3101, on the Cross City Line to Lichfield, during the early hours.
October 29th – GEC Alsthom Metro-Cammell wins £250million contract for new trains on the London Underground Jubilee Line Extension – 59 six-car sets, to be designated '1996 stock'.
December 29th – A special meeting of the WMPTA discusses a new station to serve the International Convention Centre. The PTA had budgeted £358,000 for the cost of associated signalling work, but BR had announced, without warning or explanation, that this had risen to £1.54million. The PTA felt unable to proceed and so the station was 'lost'. By December 1998 the total cost was estimated at £7.5million and the WMPTA put in a bid for a Government Transportation Grant to help finance the project. The bid was unsuccessful. This much needed station remains lost, thanks to the whim and conceit of some anonymous ex-British Rail accountant(s).

1994

February 7th – Class 323 emus enter service on the Cross City Line.
October – Transrail launches 'Enterprise'.

1995

April – Post Office sidings at Sutton Park taken out of use – removed in January 1998.
May time-table changes include withdrawal of Plymouth-Scotland sleepers through Birmingham and provision of a West Midlands HST connection to Eurostar, withdrawn from 4th January 1997.
June 19th – The Maglev link between Birmingham International Airport and station is closed.
September 25th – Jewellery Line opens.

1996

March 31st – Last day of service of Class 304 emus in Central Trains area, on Cross City Line.
July 26th – New steel terminal opens at Wolverhampton.
September – Snow Hill's Platform 4 taken out of use, awaiting Metro. Track recovered in June 1997.
September 28th – Last trains called at Smethwick West, known in GWR days as Smethwick Junction.

1997

June 2nd – Passenger service on the Chase Line extended to new station at Rugeley Town.
July 11th – Hams Hall freight terminal opened.

1998

January 10th – Refurbishment of Platform 1 at Birmingham New Street begun. The work involved new surfaces and improved lighting. This was part of Railtrack's £18million regeneration scheme for the station. Other platforms were then refurbished, in order. Work continued into 1999.
January 14th – New sidings at Walsall to cope with booming traffic at Wolverhampton Steel Terminal.
April 18th – First General Motors Class 66 freight locomotive arrives in UK.
May 24th – Walsall-Wolverhampton line re-opens to passengers.
May 25th – Chase Line services extended from Rugeley Town to Rugeley Trent Valley and Stafford.
July 14th – Derailment of steel train causes serious damage to the track at Smethwick Junction. Junction not reinstated until October!
November 18th – New Virgin Travel Centre and passenger lounge opened at Wolverhampton.

1999

May 31st – Line 1 of Midland Metro opens, mostly using the trackbed of the Great Western main line from Snow Hill to Wolverhampton. An estimated 27,000 passengers carried on this day.

Notes

The number and sheer variety of train services in the West Midlands continued to grow in the final years of the twentieth century. Some new long distance patterns were established, though others proved more temporary.

The "Birmingham Pullman" began running in 1987, at a time when Pullman travel was already in decline, largely because the differences between these luxury trains and the latest regular stock were very slight. Leaving New Street at 07.40, it called at International only and arrived at Euston at 09.09, the only train of the day to run through Coventry without stopping. The premium return fare was £52 (£60 with breakfast), against a first class return of £47. Those who paid this price really only bought half a train, as there was no return Pullman in the evening because the stock worked from Euston to Glasgow during the afternoon. Despite this it loaded well, normally in excess of 90%, but it was a non-standard train working a non-standard diagram. A Virgin West Coast train of standard stock still operates to within minutes of the original schedule, still not calling at Coventry. The 'Birmingham Pullman' footnote only disappeared from the timetables in May 1998.

The Channel Tunnel opened in 1994 and the following summer an HST was introduced between Manchester and Waterloo (arr.11.46) via Wolverhampton, Birmingham and Coventry. It connected with trains to/from Paris and Brussels before leaving Waterloo at 15.42 on its journey north. As the HST was open only to international passengers it was hopelessly uneconomic, often leaving New Street with fewer than twenty people on board. It was withdrawn in January 1997. At the time of writing the whole future of rail travel from the West Midlands to the Continent, either by connecting services or by direct Eurostars, is in serious doubt.

Yet another spoke was added to the wheel of long distance services radiating from New Street in May 1998 when Virgin Cross Country introduced three through trains a day to Guildford and Portsmouth, one of which runs to/from Blackpool North.

The 1990s have seen developments in services between the West Midlands and London, not least from Snow Hill to Marylebone since 1993. From New Street, there has been an hourly semi-fast train to Euston since electrification in 1967 but it was never meant to be used as a through service. The departure board at New Street used to show its destination as Watford Junction or even Hemel Hempstead! With privatisation it was marketed as a cheap and cheerful alternative to Virgin West Coast, with reasonable fares and fewer restrictions on travel. Traffic has grown, so there are now two Silverlink Class 321 emus per hour and the journey takes just over two hours, a little more 'fast' than 'semi'.

Through InterCity services between Euston and Shrewsbury were withdrawn in 1985, despite considerable protests. However, before 1985 there were virtually no other through trains between Shrewsbury and Birmingham; now there are two an hour.

Despite developments in the 1970s (Chapter One), there are now very few direct trains between Birmingham and Norwich. Most Birmingham-East Anglia trains take the Cambridge line at Ely and continue to Stansted Airport. Eight of them start at Wolverhampton. Norwich is served by hourly Class 170s on a lengthy cross country route (252 miles) undreamt of in the 1970s, linking the city with Liverpool via Manchester, Sheffield, Nottingham, Grantham and Peterborough. These trains connect smartly with the Birmingham service at Peterborough.

Such fast, frequent and reliable long distance services on these newly important routes would not have been possible without the Class 158 dmus. Built by BREL between 1989 and 1992, each car is fitted with a 350hp Cummins engine, providing swift acceleration and a top speed of 90mph. At first, one of their virtues brought problems; as lightweight dmus with aluminium bodyshells they cause less wear on the track, but in trial running this lack of weight frequently failed to trigger track circuits. All too often, as far as signallers were concerned, they had the nack of simply disappearing from the panel, so that nobody knew quite where they were. This was one of the teething troubles which delayed their entry into service until 1992.

Sometimes there is a lack of vision; sometimes a paranoia about safety; sometimes a plain lack of care. The 1992 proposal for a new station at Heartlands, where the Birmingham-Derby line passes under the Aston-Stechford line, was fuelled by InterCity's desire to quit New Street. The station would have been on a triangular site with new connecting spurs, a bus station, parking for 4,000 cars and probable abandonment of the Duddeston-Aston line. Most local services would have been altered to serve Heartlands. The considerable problems associated with New Street cannot be solved by transferring most of its traffic to a major station well removed from the city centre, yet much time and energy was devoted to this crazy scheme before it was abandoned in 1993. After the Kings Cross fire New Street was designated as an Underground station and an extra footbridge was opened in February 1993, for general use and as an added escape route. It does not open on Sundays, neither is there access from platforms 1 and 12. These platforms have escalators, yet they are used by some long distance trains, whose passengers are more likely to be carrying luggage. No platform at New Street is served by a down escalator and there are no plans to construct any. New Street has not been singled out for this treatment, as the escalators at Snow Hill and Birmingham International operate only in the up direction and there are no escalators at all at Coventry or Wolverhampton.

Steam age track and pointwork at Leamington Spa was replaced in the autumn of 1994, but only on a like for like basis. The opportunity to spend a little more, to invest in a more flexible layout, was lost. When the Coventry-Leamington line is doubled at some not-too-future date, it will be difficult to develop the successful Nuneaton-Coventry service by extending it through Leamington to Stratford, because the track layout still makes it virtually impossible for trains to operate through the station between the Coventry and Stratford lines. Snow Hill's Platform 4 was taken out of use in September 1996 because the alignment was need by Midland Metro. This increased congestion at the three remaining platforms, later exacerbated by the Health & Safety Executive's insistence that the well tried and perfectly safe practice of having two trains in each platform at busy times should cease because there were no signals halfway along the platforms. H&E relented in 1998. The derailment of a steel train at Galton Junction on 14th July 1998 resulted in substantial damage to the junction itself. It was repaired within days <u>but restored as plain line.</u> Birmingham-Wolverhampton trains could run, but the physical connection between New Street and the Stourbridge line was severed. Railtrack countered strong local protest with feeble excuses about the special nature of the track, explaining that delays in reconstructing the junction were due to "bespoke pointwork"! The junction was not restored until October. Had it been bombed during the Second World War it would have been in use again within days, if not hours.

In the summer of 1999, two dmus working in the West Midlands were on loan from Wales & West (Cardiff Canton) and ScotRail (Edinburgh Haymarket). The W&W unit worked to Birmingham on a time-tabled train. ScotRail have no scheduled trains to the Midlands, so Railtrack could charge for this unit's use of the track. ScotRail discovered that the proposed charge was greater than the cost of hiring two low loaders to bring the two-car unit down the motorway from Carlisle. This they did, with a repeat hire for the return trip. To any right thinking person, a charging system which forces a railway company to act in this way is simply mad!

Railtrack, of course, is one of the arms of railway management born of privatisation, the biggest upheaval the network has experienced since nationalisation in 1948. It is far beyond the scope of this book to comment at length on privatisation and it is far too soon, at the time of writing, to assess its long term effects. Certainly there are more trains and more people using them, the long decline in freight traffic has been reversed and train builders' order books are full.

Every year Railtrack publishes a document, the Network Management Statement (NMS), describing its hopes for the development of the network. The 1999 NMS, published on March 25th and running to 350 pages, predicted a 30% growth in rail traffic over the next ten years. It proposed the spending nationally of £27billion over that period but much of that money would have to be raised through 'partnership funding', ie; from councils, businesses and sources other than Railtrack itself. Key

Top Drawer Sprinter. 158 714 is seen during a proving run on the Birmingham West Suburban Line, approaching the site of Somerset Road station on its way to New Street, 24th July 1990. *(John Boynton)*

During the summer of 1999, the (SO) 12.10 Ramsgate-Glasgow was often hauled by a Deltic (!) as far as New Street. D9000 has arrived at Saltley for servicing after working this train, 17th July 1999. *(Maurice Newman)*

Galton Junction, 14th July 1998. The overnight 23.41 Lackenby (Tees-side) – Wolverhampton Steel Terminal was derailed at 06.14, causing serious damage to the track and to the pointwork at the junction. The eastbound carriageway of the adjacent A457 was closed to allow heavy lifting cranes in to move the damaged wagons away. Here, loco No.60 080 has been brought in to move the derailed wagons to the crane. Subsequent investigations over the train's route as far back as Water Orton established that at least one vehicle in the train had derailed at Ryecroft Junction, and again at Perry Barr, damaging sleepers and scoring the rail before 'bouncing back' and re-railing itself. The Stour Valley route was restored as plain line within three days; the pointwork at the junction was not replaced untl October!
(Stephen Widdowson)

infrastructure proposals for the West Midlands can be summarised thus:–

- Quadruple 10 miles of the Birmingham-Coventry line, between Stechford and Berkswell, at a cost of £200m.
- Quadruple the Birmingham-Wolverhampton line between Monument Lane and Dudley Port to increase capacity for local trains from two to four per hour. Centro to bear the cost, Centro unwilling to do so (the improvement would benefit all users of the line, so why should just one user pay?) therefore this route is likely to remain double track.
- Double the remaining 8 miles of single track between Snow Hill and Marylebone, from Aynho Junction to Bicester.
- Walsall-Brownhills is listed only as a possible candidate for re-opening as the trackbed is not owned by Railtrack.
- Walsall-Stourbridge re-opening is complicated by a possible extension of the Metro along the same alignment, with shared tracks. Possible re-opening is costed at £75m for 2006.
- Electrification is suggested between Walsall and Rugeley (£35m for 2005), along the Sutton Park Line and between New Street and Nuneaton, mainly to benefit freight (£50m for 2002).

None of these desirable schemes will definitely happen, all are dependent on partnership funding from councils, etc. Only time will tell ....

87 007 "City of Manchester" with a northbound InterCity service. Thomas Telford's 'Main Line' Canal is to the right. The up and down goods loops are invaluable on this congested stretch of railway. Tipton gas works was still extant at the time, March 1987.*(David Pagett)*

A Class 310 four-car emu arrives at Dudley Port with the 14.30 New Street-Wolverhampton, 19th October 1974. The weights by the mast help keep the overhead in tension. The platform seat is a relic of the LNWR. *(Michael Mensing)*

30th July 1987 and the new through station at Birmingham Moor Street is nearing completion, with the refurbished Snow Hill Tunnel beyond. To the right, the dark blue bricks form part of the cutting retaining wall for the lines out of the London end of New Street. The old Moor Street is already sprouting weeds. *(courtesy of Centro)*

Passengers once More

Since 1987 five lines have re-opened to passengers in the West Midlands.

WMPTA had agreed, in principle, to reinstate services between Kidderminster and Leamington via Snow Hill in 1973. By 1982 West Midlands County Council had allocated £165,000 for research into the scheme. 'Modern Railways' (August 1982) reported :– *"Local and County Councillors representing areas which would be served by the proposed line are enthusiastic about the scheme and the Chairman of the County Passenger Transport Committee, Councillor Philip Bateman, has said that the new rail link would help regenerate industry along the route.... Proponents of the project point to the success of the Longbridge-Four Oaks cross-city line to support their case. No costs have been put forward for the Stourbridge-Solihull line but it is estimated that the restoration of Snow Hill Tunnel would cost about £7million. A ten year time scale is estimated for the project."*

The West Midlands County Council, along with all others in England and Wales, had to submit a Transport Policy and Programme (TPP) annually to central government, outlining proposed projects and seeking government approval and a share of funding in the form of a government grant, a Transport Supplementary Grant. These were not distributed lightly. The Snow Hill scheme was included in each year's TPP from 1979 to 1983 without success, but in 1983 the Department of Transport approved the first phase of the scheme with a grant under Section 56 of the 1968 Transport Act. Phase One provided for new stations at Moor Street and Snow Hill, re-opening of the tunnel and closure of the old Moor Street. Work commenced in 1985. An accumulation of soot up to six inches thick was removed from the walls of the tunnel. The tough blue brickwork was generally found to be in excellent condition. New tracks within the tunnel were laid with rubber padding beneath the sleepers to minimise vibrations. High visibility sodium lighting was installed. A new station at Moor Street, with two full length side platforms, took shape at the tunnel approach. Snow Hill was provided with two full length island platforms, which sit beneath a multi-storey car park. The station's 'architecture' is functional rather than inspiring, for which Birmingham City Council is to blame. The council decided to build the car park where it is, delaying the station's opening by six months and blighting its appearance.

Before opening day, the general public were given an opportunity to walk through the 596 yard tunnel. On Saturday 12th September 1987 queues formed at the old Moor Street before opening at 9.30am. Walkers were to give a minimum donation of 50p to local charities. They were led by the Lord Mayor of Birmingham, Councillor Fred Grattidge. By mid-afternoon the queue at Moor Street was over a mile long and by the end of the day over 14,000 people had walked the tunnel, all of whom received a certificate when emerging onto the platforms at Snow Hill.

On Friday 2nd October the first train into Snow Hill was hauled by 47 484 "Isambard Kingdom Brunel", with the Chairman of British Rail on board, en route to a celebratory banquet at the Grand Hotel. The following day another special carried the new Bishop of Birmingham, Rev.Mark Santer, commuting from Moor Street to Snow Hill - from a special service at St.Martin's in the Bull Ring to his enthronement in St.Philip's Cathedral. Public services began on Monday 5th October. Consultation of the time-table showed that it was possible to catch the first train out of Snow Hill as far as Moor Street and there join the first train into Snow Hill. This I did, along with several dozen other people, to be greeted on re-arrival at Snow Hill by BR and WMPTE officials bearing glasses of champagne and the obligatory certificate.

Some of the 14,052 people who walked through Snow Hill tunnel arrive at journey's end, Saturday 12th September 1987. This was a unique opportunity to walk the 596 yard tunnel, which had last seen a passenger train on 2nd March 1968, and each walker donated a minimum of 50p to charity. The Lord Mayor of Birmingham sent off the first walkers from the old Moor Street station and BRMB disc jockey Les Ross broadcast from within the tunnel. All those who completed the walk received a commemorative certificate. During the afternoon the queue to join the walk grew longer than a mile, and some latecomers had to be turned away. *(Stephen Widdowson)*

Snow Hill station in pristine condition. The platform clock, radio controlled from Rugby, shows 10.32 as Tyseley set T307 waits to leave with a service to Shirley. Notice the subtle black girder. *(courtesy of Centro)*

Smethwick Galton Bridge, upper level, with 150 109 bound for Snow Hill and beyond (even though the destination blind reads 'Stourbridge Junction'), 5th October 1995. The Stour Valley platforms lie beneath, and the link between New Street and the Stourbridge line can be glimpsed beyond the bridge. The flats, for long a local landmark, have since been demolished. *(John Whitehouse)*

Snow Hill station is in a prime city centre location, ideally placed for the business district. This was one important factor which contributed to the success of the new service. The WMPTA had always had a positive attitude to rail. The success of the Cross City Line, and now Snow Hill, only reinforced that and they were quick to lodge a Bill in Parliament, in 1988, for re-opening to Smethwick – what would later be known as the Jewellery Line. As with Stage I, this was the first of many hurdles. The Department of Transport did not approve the scheme until 1992, even then warning that none of its money could be made available and that the proposed new station at Galton Bridge would not add to the scheme's benefits! They held out the crumb of a £5million grant from the European Regional Development Fund if contracts were let by the end of the year. They were, and the Minister for Public Transport, Roger Freeman, inaugurated work at the controls of a JCB digger at Snow Hill on 28th January 1993. The £20m budget was exceeded when construction was advancing in the spring of 1994, just as – on 1st April – privatisation meant that responsibility for BR's financial contribution and completion of the project passed to Railtrack. In the ensuing public debate, Railtrack threatened to put contracts for final parts of the scheme 'on hold' unless Centro increased its financial contribution; Centro countered by threatening to withhold all its share. For a moment the scheme seemed in doubt, but that was an illusion sponsored by the media scenting a 'good' story. The parties compromised, Centro paying a further £1.86m. The total estimated cost had risen to £25.72m, so Railtrack agreed to foot the bill for any costs beyond that.

The line opened on 25th September 1995, preceeded by a Gala Day on Sunday 24th, when a shuttle service had been provided between Snow Hill and Stourbridge, hauled by BR Standard tank 80079, on loan from the SVR. There are four off peak trains per hour between Snow Hill and Stourbridge, two all stations and two semi-fast. A fifth train serves New Street, the terminus for all Stourbridge Line trains before 1995. The three new stations at Jewellery Quarter, The Hawthorns and Smethwick Galton Bridge, are well designed, well built, light and user-friendly. Jewellery Quarter and Galton Bridge feature large areas of coloured glass. The Hawthorns has a free car park and interchange with the Metro. Galton Bridge, the most expensive to build at £4m, has platforms on the Jewellery and Stour Valley lines. Its potential as an interchange station is slowly building as more passengers from the Snow Hill lines now realise that it is easy to change here for direct trains to New Street, Coventry and Wolverhampton. All three stations are fully staffed and fitted with CCTV.

The Coventry-Nuneaton line had closed to passengers in 1965, but it remained in use for freight and as an important diversionary route. On the initiative of BR Provincial, passenger services were restored on an experimental basis on 11th May 1987. There was a handful of trains a day, provided by a single unit bubble car. The intermediate station at Bedworth opened in May 1988. The prospect of new Sprinter stock for Birmingham-East Anglia trains prompted plans to gain further passengers by diverting them via Coventry, where they would reverse on their way to/from Nuneaton. These plans, 'pencilled in' by BR's Provincial sector for 1988, were abandoned when the implications of channelling more trains along the congested Birmingham-Coventry line had been considered. In fact, the Coventry-Nuneaton line did not need the support of these extra trains. Traffic built up and today there is an hourly service linking Coventry directly with Nuneaton, Leicester and Nottingham.

The Cross City Line gained an extra station when the high level platforms at Lichfield Trent Valley were re-opened on 28th November 1988. It has attracted custom from commuters living north of the city because it is easy to drive to and has an adequate car park. The New Street-Lichfield route was earmarked for electrification in 1967 but it fell victim to false economies. The whole Cross City Line was eventually electrified in the 1990s. Work began in May 1990 and a full electric service started in July 1993. WMPTA had advocated electrification since 1980 but it was not easy convincing the Department of Transport that this, the busiest diesel commuter line in the world, was a suitable case

Sprinter 150 123 calls at Jewellery Quarter with the 15.05 Leamington Spa-Kidderminster service on 3rd October 1995.
(John Whitehouse)

Smethwick West on the last day of service, 28th September 1996, as 150 120 passes en route to Stourbridge Junction. This station became surplus to requirements when Galton Bridge opened in 1995, just round the left curve. A 'bureaucratic hiccup' delayed closure for a year, during which there was one train a week (SO) in each direction.
(John Whitehouse)

for treatment. By 1989 the line was carrying 30,000 passengers a day and the heritage dmus were reaching the end of their lives. An electrification scheme was jointly submitted by the PTA and the British Railways Board to the Department of Transport in November 1988. There followed a whole year in which the department denied ever having received the submission! Having finally agreed he had indeed received a submission, the Secretary of State for Transport, Cecil Parkinson, wrote to the PTA and BRB on 2nd November 1989 saying, *"I am afraid I cannot give immediate approval for electrification of this line, although I hope to do so in due course."* He had called for evaluations comparing the cost of electric trains with the cost of new diesel trains and was awaiting the outcome. This sounded like another stalling tactic. The MP for Mid-Staffordshire died that autumn, forcing a by-election. The constituency's southern boundary was Blake Street station. At the 1987 election John Heddle's majority was 14,654, one of the safest seats in the country. The government was suffering a period of unpopularity and seemed likely to lose the by-election. On 7th February 1990, in the middle of the campaign, Cecil Parkinson gave approval for electrification of the line. The government still lost the seat.

Cross City electrification included purpose built electric multiple units, the Class 323, supplied by Hunslet of Leeds. They are comfortable and reliable commuter trains, but they had considerable teething troubles. They were delivered late, the first arriving in February 1994, seven months after electrification was complete. That summer the door mechanisms suffered in the heat but worse was to come when frosty autumn weather shut traction converters down for no obvious reason. The low point was the morning peak of October 5th, when four 323s stalled near Blake Street. It eventually transpired that the traction converter could not differentiate between the natural arcing on the overhead caused by the frost and currents which were potentially hazardous to the unit's infrastructure so, for safety's sake, it shut all systems down. Once the converters had been programmed to recognise the arcing 'signature' the problem was solved. Nowadays the 323s have achieved at least 92% availability (Class 323 Paper published by the Institution of Mechanical Engineers in 'Journal of Rail and Rapid Transit', 1999 Vol.213 No.F1).

The Walsall-Rugeley line re-opened in three stages. Talks were held between Cannock District Council and British Rail as early as 1970, the first of many such discussions with local authorities. By 1984 a £20,000 feasibility study, financed by BR, confirmed that a service was practical. West Midlands County Council agreed to help fund the re-opening but Staffordshire County Council did not, despite having been presented with a five thousand name petition earlier the same year. For the financial year 1985/86 they did earmark £197,000 for the three proposed stations within the county. Although this was only 1.3% of the county's total transport budget, it was withdrawn when the overall budget was trimmed. Finally, in October 1988, a package was agreed. The cost of re-opening between Walsall and Hednesford, with stations at Bloxwich, Broad Lane, Landywood, Cannock and Hednesford, was £500,000, of which £230,000 was contributed by WMPTE and £200,000 by Staffordshire. The service began on 10th April 1989. There was an hourly shuttle between Hednesford and Walsall, with one train to New Street in the morning and an evening return. In 1991 all trains began running through to Birmingham.

Bloxwich station was built north of the town centre, the cheap but inconvenient option. There are proposals to close it and build a new station on the original site. Bloxwich North (named Broad Lane at the planning stage) opened late, in October 1990, because of problems with land acquisition. No new station was provided at Wyrley and Cheslyn Hay (1858-1965) but a halt with staggered platforms was erected three quarters of a mile south at Landywood, where an earlier halt had closed at the end of 1915. Nothing remained of Cannock station, but a halt was built on the same site. The surviving southbound platform at Hednesford was brought back into use. All stations have car parks, except Bloxwich. All stations were provided with basic platforms and Amsted 'Clifton' waiting shelters. All were unstaffed and prone to vandalism, Landywood suffering a grafitti attack on the morning of opening day.

South of Walsall, a park-and-ride station opened at Tame Bridge in June 1990, alongside the A4031 Walsall-West Bromwich road. Difficulties with land acquisition delayed construction of the 233 space car park until 1996, since when it has been known as Tame Bridge Parkway. There are now four trains an hour between New Street and Walsall, two of which are fast, calling only at Tame Bridge.

On 2nd June 1997 the train service was extended from Hednesford – which was given a new northbound platform – to a new station at Rugeley Town. (The route was now marketed as 'The Chase Line' because it runs over Cannock Chase.) This was just a stepping stone to the final extension, which occurred on 25th May 1998, when trains began running through to Rugeley Trent Valley and Stafford. There was a Press Trip on 18th May during which speeches were made at Stafford, Rugeley Trent Valley and Walsall. The Chairman of Staffordshire County Council, Cllr.Roger Wright, said, *"We were convinced that the link was worthwhile. The service from Birmingham to Rugeley has exceeded expectations and amply justified investment."* Mark Causebrook, MD of Central Trains, pointed to a 12% growth in rail passengers in the West Midlands over the previous twelve months adding, *"We are riding on the crest of a wave with the opening of the Chase Line"* while Cllr.Richard Worrall, Chair of WMPTA, reminded everyone that Walsall was no longer at the end of a branch line. He would like to see a halt for hikers on the Chase at Morse Gorse Crossing. As to what happened next, *"Electrification is the big one"*. Another prospect for the line is construction of the proposed parkway station at Churchbridge, adjacent to the A5.

The Chase Line Press Trip on 18th May was one of a pair. The following day councillors and other invitees assembled again, this time at Wolverhampton, for a pre-opening special over the electrified freight line to Walsall. On arrival at Walsall the train was greeted by the Mayor, Cllr.Bill Newman. This was his first official duty, having been elected the previous evening. (The last duty of his predecessor, Cllr.Norman Matthews, had been to welcome guests aboard the Chase Line special at Stafford). Councillor Judith Rowley of WMPTA officially launched the service, whilst Cllr.Richard Worrall hoped that it would soon be extended at both ends. For the first week a special fare of 10p applied and trains were full. Stock varied from a 323 to the more usual Class 153 single unit. Between 1958 and 1965, dmus ran hourly between Wolverhampton and Walsall, alternate trains going forward to Burton-on-Trent via Brownhills and Lichfield. However, apart from Sundays, the new service is not at regular intervals. They run every 40 minutes - more or less - not at times which are easy to carry around in the head. The line itself is stationless, but there are hopes for a station at Willenhall. The big advantage enjoyed by the train over the parallel congested roads is a journey time of just 12 minutes, half that by bus even in ideal conditions. Once this is allied to a clock face time-table the service will probably be as successful as other West Midland re-openings of recent years.

Newly electrified Cross City Line; shame about the train. The 10.09 from New Street to Lichfield Trent Valley approaches Burton Old Road Crossing, between Lichfield's two stations, Sunday 31st March 1996. The train consists of two Class 304 sets, 304 033 and 304 002. These were built for local traffic on the first part of the WCML to be electrified, Crewe-Manchester/Liverpool, in 1960. They were originally non-corridor four-car sets, converted to three-car opens during the 1980s. After more than 35 years service, fit only for the knacker's yard, some 304 sets carried out last gasp duties on the Cross City Line while the 323s were – at length – obtaining a clean bill of health. This was the last day 304s operated on the line. *(Roger Shenton)*

You can't bring that piano in here! The new one-tonne signalling console for the northern part of the Cross City Line is squeezed into the ex-Vauxhall Shunt Frame signal box, 9.30am, Sunday 7th June 1992. The box was renamed Aston Signalling Centre and from this console the signaller controls the 54 colour light signals between Aston and Lichfield Trent Valley. After Saltley and New Street this is Birmingham's third power box, and the only one not situated on a route under its control. The box was built in 1957, with a standard London Midland Region frame (4½" between the lever centres), later reduced to a capacity of 20 levers. It was re-windowed in 1991, ready for conversion to its new role. *(courtesy of Centro)*

Tame Bridge station, with a Walsall-New Street Class 310 emu, seen from the aqueduct of the Tame Valley Canal, part of the Birmingham Canal Navigations. The station opened on 4th June 1990. To the rear are the masts of Bescot Yard. The distinctive RAC control room is sited north of Junction 8 on the M6. Difficulties with land acquisition delayed the construction of the station's 233-space car park. After that was completed, in 1996, the station was re-named Tame Bridge Parkway and all trains between Birmingham and Walsall – four per hour off-peak – now call. *(courtesy of Centro)*

A warm summer morning as Sprinter 150 010 breaks the banner at Rugeley Town, 30th May 1997. This was a VIP special, followed by a gala weekend after which, as the banner proclaims, normal services began on 2nd June. Rugeley Power Station, coal fired and rail served, forms a backdrop. *(Roger Shenton)*

Councillors Richard Worrall and Judith Rowley flank Rob Donald, Director General of Centro, after the arrival of the pre-opening Wolverhampton-Walsall special, 19th May 1998.
(John Boynton)

Some stations which escaped the Beeching axe had their train services reduced to almost nothing. They endured long years of impotent suspended animation, in a state of virtual closure. The worst example was Bromsgrove, where the entire service consisted of one train to Birmingham in the morning and an evening return. BR took the Minister of Transport, Tom Fraser, too literally when he refused closure in 1965 and stipulated that a minimum commuter service must run. The Bromsgrove Passenger Action Committee, which had fought hard against closure, was now fighting just as hard to improve this insulting 'service'. Representations to the next Minister of Transport, Barbara Castle, succeeded in getting a second evening train to call. By 1969 Bromsgrove commuters had the support of the TUCC for further improvements, but their case fell on deaf ears. They did not know about impending alterations to the track through the station. The southbound platform was on a loop off the through line. The kink in the main line, through the station and at the foot of the Lickey Incline, was to be ironed out to allow faster running. The platform loop and the platform itself were to be removed. The southbound track was to be slewed about six feet and raised about three feet. BR did not want the expense of building a new station for so few trains. Closure would have been a much cheaper option, but because of the strong support for the Action Committee from the TUCC, BR compromised by retaining the northbound platform. Southbound trains calling at Bromsgrove used the new crossover near the foot of the incline, travelling 'wrong round' before crossing back a little further south. Remarkably, the station was staffed 24 hours a day, chiefly in connection with the crews manning the banking engines.

Improvements began in earnest with five extra trains a day in 1979, thanks to financial support from Hereford & Worcester County Council. The train service fluctuated over the next few years. A very few long distance trains called here but their number and timings varied with each time-table change. From an operational point of view it was difficult and uneconomic to stop such trains at the foot of the Incline. In 1989 an attempt was made to improve the Bromsgrove service with a single unit bubble car, which shuttled between Worcester and Barnt Green, where passengers changed for Birmingham. This again attracted support from the county council, which also sponsored the new southbound platform, which opened in May 1990. Bromsgrove at last had a proper station once more. A new Birmingham-Worcester-Cardiff service had started in 1987, with Class 150 Sprinters. In 1988 it transferred to the Bromsgrove route and with provision of the new platform a few of these trains began calling there to supplement the bubble car, which was gradually phased out. Bromsgrove now enjoys an approximately hourly service, courtesy of Central Trains and Wales & West, which jointly run a Cardiff-Birmingham-Nottingham service. Even when there was only a single train each way, up to forty people used Bromsgrove station. The number of regular commuters is now approaching four hundred. Trains take about 25 minutes to New Street and morning peak departures are at 06.12, 07.25, 07.45, 07.50 and 08.08, during which time Bromsgrove is 'staffed' once more, by a railman issuing tickets from a portable machine. The station car park is in urgent need of expansion and some space has been earmarked on the town side of the station, near where the stationmaster's house once stood. Bromsgrove now enjoys the best train service it has ever had. It is less spectacular than holiday expresses up the Lickey, banked by Big Bertha, but it is far more use to the local people.

Metro-Cammell built 156 411 waits to depart from Bromsgrove's new platform with the 12.21 to Cardiff, 22nd May 1990.
(John Boynton)

Freight

The most serious single loss to freight in the West Midlands in recent years has been the closure as a through route of the Walsall-Dudley-Stourbridge Line in 1993. Together with the Walsall-Lichfield Line, this important freight route served Bescot Yard and by-passed Birmingham. The whole was a straightforward and relatively easily graded line, the most direct link between Bescot and the East Midlands/NE England via Lichfield, and SW England/South Wales via Dudley. Northbound freight from Bescot now uses the Sutton Park Line - indirect, steeply graded and congested, with low line speeds due to the condition of the track. Southbound trains take a variety of routes, none of them straightforward.

The section north of Lichfield, to the junction with the Birmingham-Derby main line at Wichnor, still sees some freight, which uses the connecting spur at Lichfield to reach the Trent Valley Line. Between Lichfield and Brownhills the remaining single line serves the oil depot at Brownhills and is used by no more than three trains a week. There is a four mile gap between Brownhills and Ryecroft Junction, Walsall. Part of the trackbed is in short term use by lorries accessing an opencast mine near Pelsall. The whole trackbed is protected from encroachment or development and, at the time of writing, both the freight company EWS (English Welsh & Scottish Railway) and WMPTA are considering the feasibility of restoring the railway.

South of Walsall the line is disused between Pleck Junction and Round Oak. Short sections of track have now been lifted, across Parkhead viaduct and in its vicinity. The double track north from Stourbridge Junction serves the steel terminals at Brierley Hill and Round Oak. The line ends short of the A4036, just beyond Round Oak Rail, a thriving terminal served by daily trains from Margam and Boston. Round Oak opened on the initiative of Railfreight, who were determined to capture a larger share of the West Midlands steel market. The government made a Section 8 grant payment in 1984 of £1.15m to help set up the facility ('Modern Railways', May 1987). There is a large covered area served by three rail lines. It is heated, a necessary expense to keep cold reduced coil in ex-works condition, because this coated steel is vulnerable to rusting if exposed to cool or damp before processing. Brierley Hill terminal closed in May 1997, only to re-open two months later as steel traffic continued to grow. Some trains to these terminals now consist of covered vans with a distinctive profile. Their steel hoods are in three sections, the two smaller ones sliding, as in a telescope, beneath the largest one when they are opened. The vans are each designed to carry up to 100 tonnes of steel coil and the first one, part of an order from EWS, emerged from Thrall Europa's York works in July 1998, two months early.

There is considerable uncertainty over the line's long term future. As with the Walsall-Lichfield section, WMPTA is anxious to reintroduce passenger services. In 1997 Railtrack proposed lifting the track on Bescot Curve, the line's link with Bescot Yard. This would have economised on the urgently needed re-equipping of Walsall power box. Although the curve would not be used by passenger trains, WMPTA saw this as unhelpful and objected vigorously, compelling Railtrack to withdraw. Between Wednesbury and some as yet undecided point near Round Oak, it is proposed that a reinstated railway should share its tracks with a second Metro line, which would leave Line 1 at Wednesbury to serve the large shopping centre at Merry Hill. Whether it is possible to run heavy freight trains, passenger trains and frequent Metro trams on the same pair of tracks and provide a good service for all these very different customers, must be open to doubt. Whilst it is technically feasible, my opinion is that freight and passenger trains on this line could mix well, but the added ingredient of the Metro would cause problems for all users. Metro running frequently would delay other traffic; Metro running infrequently would not be a proper Metro. Metro with few stops on the railway, so as not to impede the trains, could not be used by people living near it. It needs a separate formation because Metro is not a train and should not be made to act like one.

Speedlink, the wagonload distribution network axed in 1991, was succeeded when Transrail launched 'Enterprise' at Warrington on 5th September 1994. For efficient and economic working, there was to be less marshalling and trip working than there had been with Speedlink. The first service consisted of an overnight route linking Wembley, Bescot, Warrington, Mossend, Aberdeen and Elgin.

One cliche describes the nature of West Midlands industry as 'metal bashing'. The metal to be 'bashed' is predominantly steel and recent years have seen rail play an increasing role in bringing it into the region for further distribution and processing. New flows have been created - imported steel is now railed in via the re-opened rail link at the docks in Boston, Lincolnshire. The biggest and busiest steel terminal in the region is at Wolverhampton, on the east side of the Stour Valley Line. It was enlarged at a cost of £1.4m and the new building opened on 26th July 1996. This is an EWS terminal and at the opening ceremony two wagons were included in that day's train from Tees-side which were the first to be painted in the now familiar EWS maroon livery. Traffic has continued to grow and it regularly overflows the site, spilling under the main line into the formerly disused Chillington Wharf. The wharf buildings are decaying, the track is choked with weeds, the canal has seen no commercial traffic for decades, but the sidings bustle with the growl of an 08 loco shunting bogie bolster wagons loaded with steel bars. Two sidings were even opened at Walsall in April 1998 to deal with the Wolverhampton overspill.

On 1st April 1999 I was allowed access to the Freightliner Terminal at Birmingham Lawley Street, guided by Colin Hunt, the shift manager. This is one of the older Freightliner yards, on a confined site south-east of the city centre, secured with high pallisade fencing and CCTV. It is dominated by the two 40 tonne Morris gantry cranes, erected in 1991-2. Bright yellow, they are clearly visible from trains on the Cross City and Euston lines. The yard is open 24 hours a day, except for the weekend shutdown between 2pm on Saturdays and 6am on Mondays. The cranes are active almost continuously, day and night, pausing only for crew changes. Their drivers are in radio contact with each other and with the control building.

Six lines are available within the terminal, each with a capacity of 17 Freightliner wagons, or flats. The gantry cranes straddle these lines on tracks of their own, constantly moving to and fro, lifting and transferring containers. The confined site has caused problems until recently due to the inadequate length of the neck beyond the locomotive run round loop. One loco could bring a train in, detach and draw ahead to the buffers, having just enough room to reverse onto the loop and be released. However, with double headed trains, which are becoming more common, both locos were marooned at the head of their train until a third came across from Saltley depot to pull the train away and release them. Track extension now means that two locos can fit beyond the end of the run round loop.

The yard has services to such destinations as Tilbury, Isle of Grain, Seaforth, Crewe, Southampton and Felixstowe. The Felixstowe trains in particular run to capacity and sometimes reliefs are required. There are about ten trains in and out every day. Main services consist of whole trains direct to their destinations, but an interesting exception is the 19.57 (4K50)

In the years just prior to closure of the Stourbridge-Dudley-Walsall line, its most notable working was the Tuesdays only engineers train from Gloucester to Bescot, diagrammed for a Class 50. 50 004 "St.Vincent" crosses Parkhead Viaduct at Blowers Green, 25th April 1989. The poor condition of this viaduct was given as one reason for closure of the line. It was said that old ballast had not been removed when life-expired. New ballast was simply laid on top of it, adding to the weight the viaduct had to bear. Certainly, from this angle, the accumulated ballast makes it appear as though the wagons are travelling along the parapet! *(John Whitehouse)*

66 099 at Snead's Green, Hartlebury, with a rake of 'Thrall Hoods' on train 6V07, the empties from Round Oak to Margam, 2nd September 1999. *(Bob Sweet)*

Lawley Street. A general view of the terminal, showing an old and new gantry crane, seen from the other old one. To the right there is a block of stacked empties and a newly concreted lorry turning area, which is now used for stacking, the lorries turning to the right, out of the picture. Containers of various heights and lengths await the attention of the cranes. Some of the container 'flats' are partly empty, showing their skeletal nature. To the rear is the old Wright's Hemp Rope Works, now used for storage. *(Colin Hunt)*

departure to Crewe (Basford Hall). It normally carries flats for five destinations, Coatbridge, Tilbury, Isle of Grain, Seaforth and Purfleet. It may carry flats for other destinations 'as required' and the train is split at Crewe. Each train out loads up to a maximum of 25 flats. Each 60' flat is designed to carry a 40' and 20' container, three 20' containers or two of 30'. The safe maximum load per flat is 58 tonnes. Each service has its upper weight limit.

Containers have three standard heights, 8'6", 9', 9'6", and some routes have height restrictions. Southampton trains have to use special low flats, which are also six feet longer than the others and coupled in sets of four. As each train leaves the terminal it passes through a beam, which sounds an alarm if an overheight container has been included in error.

Terminal staff are not normally aware of the contents of containers, that is part of customer confidentiality. The terminal handles traffic for major shipping agents, such as P&O and Maersk and container users are their customers. All imports are custom cleared at the docks. Lawley Street concentrates on deep sea traffic; containers to/from Europe via the Channel Tunnel are handled at Hams Hall and Daventry.

One corner of the site, near Viaduct Street, houses the container repair workshop. Any container needing repair, interior cleaning or inspection is tagged and taken for stacking near the shed by one of three mobile cranes constantly at work within the terminal. After repair, each container is craned into another appropriate stack, from which it can be taken for use at short notice. Rail freight has been handled hereabouts without a break since 1842, when the Birmingham & Derby Junction Railway opened its Lawley Street terminus, for passengers and goods, in the confined space between the Grand Junction and London & Birmingham lines converging on Curzon Street. This original site lies east of Lawley Middleway, which is a good place from which to see the original Grand Junction Viaduct, with its LNW replacement of 1893 riding piggy-back on top.

Freight handling at Hams Hall, on the site of the old power station and accessed from Whitacre Junction, began on 11th July 1997. Deputy Prime Minister John Prescott flagged away the first train, after naming loco 47 312 "Parsec of Europe". I was shown round in March 1999 by David Webb, the yard manager, who explained that Parsec runs about fifty terminals in the USA. This is their first venture into Europe. The site is ideally situated, close to Birmingham but without local road congestion, and with easy access to M6 and M42. As at Lawley Street, it is fully secure, with high fencing and CCTV. There are three long sidings. At most yards the siding nearest the main line is numbered 1, but here it is numbered 3. There is space for two more sidings between 3 and the main line, so these can be laid at

A Lawley Street gantry crane lifts a container from a lorry by four legs which grip it by means of the continous 'pocket' or ridge running along its sides. The crane driver's cab is just visible above the container. *(Colin Hunt)*

some future date without having to re-number the others.

The freight terminal forms only a part of the Hams Hall Park site. Large companies are establishing a presence at the Park, creating opportunities for Parsec. Birds Eye have a large frozen food plant and BMW have built a plant for their Rover engines. Both have the option of a rail link to the freight terminal, in which case Parsec could send a team over for the arrival and departure of their trains and service the site for them. The Rover plant is 1½ miles away by road but only 500 yards as the crow flies. If the option of a direct rail link is not adopted – which seems likely – firms within the Park should still be attracted by the facilities at the rail terminal. As David said, *"Their own sidings look doubtful, but I believe they'll still come through us because we can bring things in to firms on site without touching the congested motorway network"*.

Containers arriving by rail have come through the Channel Tunnel on various trains. They are remarshalled at the European Freight Operations Centre, Wembley. In the spring of 1999 there were five trains a day, two arrivals from Wembley at 04.20 and 10.15, with three departures at 14.18, 20.38 and 23.05. The terminal closes after the 14.18 departure on Saturdays and re-opens at 4am on Mondays. Most lorries delivering and collecting containers do so within a radius of twenty miles. David recognised one particular lorry, whose owner-driver sometimes makes three trips to the terminal in a day, *"He can do that comfortably here, much easier than when he used Lawley Street and got stuck in the traffic"*. The terminal has a long service road, which acts as a lorry park at busy times, avoiding congestion on public roads.

The site is serviced by two large mobile cranes, costing £⅓ m each. They look rather like giant menacing insects prowling up and down the wide concrete apron alongside the sidings, their 'tentacles' ready to grab any unsuspecting container. Some containers are lifted by means of twist locks inserted through holes in their top corners. This is skilled work, which can be made to look easy in the hands of an experienced crane driver. It is hard at first but a novice driver soon learns how to align crane and container, just as new car drivers learn to find marks on the bonnet to position themselves correctly on the road. If container and crane are aligned more or less accurately, one, then both twist locks at one end will find their holes. If these two fit in, the other two certainly will and the load is ready to be lifted. The other method of lifting, for other types of container, is for four 'feet' on the crane to grip the container by the inverted ridge which runs along the base of its side. This ridge has a depth of only 6mm. It can become worn and even more shallow with use, so the crane's grip is not always fully secure.

David emphasised the importance of loading the container wagons, the 'flats' or 'platforms' correctly. A 60' flat would have room for two 30' containers, but they would probably be too heavy. Just one container on a flat needs to be positioned in the middle for good weight distribution.

On site rail movements are handled by an 08 shunter (08 543 on the day of my visit) and controlled by the terminal's own small signal box, worked as required by a member of the terminal staff, its panel linked to Saltley for transfer to and from the main line. From the signal box it is possible to appreciate the size of the whole Hams Hall Park site, most of it looking more 'green fields' than former power station land. Having delivered their trains from Wembley, main line locos depart light engine for Saltley, until it is time for the return journey. Most trains are hauled by General Motors' built Class 66s, the first of which arrived in this country in April 1998. So, what are they like to drive?

I asked Ray Churchill, based at Bescot. He began by referring to two other modern freight types, the Class 60 and the Class 58. *"Although their availability is not always good, from a driver's point of view the Class 60 is excellent in almost every respect. It will pull anything, although it may be slow to accelerate, it has very good adhesion and is one of the quietest locos there is. The 58 is good on a dry rail, but terrible for slipping on a wet rail, especially with a heavy coal train. They are good passenger locos – they will streak along – although they are only used on specials or in emergencies."*

The 66s have had teething troubles. A week before our June

One of Hams Hall's mobile cranes is about to load a container onto the afternoon train to Wembley, 08 543 'in attendance'. 16th March 1999. *(John Boynton)*

1999 conversation, Ray had been on an Avonmouth mgr train when the loco failed because of a malfunction with the slow speed control, which is computer set for $^{1}/_{2}$mph. He had to return to Bescot light engine. The 66s are disappointingly noisy, especially at full throttle, a fault attributed to the engine mountings. Efforts are being made to correct this. From outside they are not noisy at all, the sound is close to a purr, but in the cab the engine noise can be intense. However, *"They have the best driving seat any loco has ever had, because they are infinitely adjustable. Most other driving seats are uncomfortable, if not at first then certainly after two hours."*

The Class 66s have standard features undreamt of even a few years ago. They are equipped with self-steering bogies which make for ease of working in the yard, with minimal wear and no squeal on the flanges. Fuel intake is metered by computer *"according to the load behind"* and, to date, Ray has never seen a 66 giving off a dark exhaust. At the start of his shift the driver uses the cab data input device, the Q-Tron Datacord Recorder, entering his personal pin number, the train reporting number and the train length. The Datacord has the same function as a black box flight recorder, registering the train speed, where it accelerates or brakes, when the aws is cancelled, etc. If the information is needed for any reason a traction inspector can come with another machine, plug it in and download data from the Datacord, converting it into script. The fact that the Datacord 'knows' the length of the train at the start of a shift is very useful, especially when travelling over a temporary slack. The Datacord always increases the length for safety's sake, thus Ray's 1080 foot long mgr train had a computerised length of 1133 feet. On approaching the T board at the end of a slack, the driver presses a button twice, starting a countdown (which also appears on a small screen) so that when the rear of the train is clear of the slack there is an electronic bleep, and the driver can accelerate to train speed.

When asked whether there were many 66s at Bescot, Ray found it difficult to answer because locos are no longer 'shedded' as such, there is a pool and they go where they are needed, sometimes at short notice. The sheds have become traction maintenance depots (TMDs). Nevertheless, Bescot will always have a share of new freight locos because it is a first rank freight TMD, very important for coal and steel traffic. The South Staffordshire Coalfield may no longer have pits, but there are heavy flows of imported coal from Avonmouth to Rugeley and Ironbridge power stations.

The Enterprise network has expanded enormously since it began, with feeder workings which include some Round Oak and Wolverhampton steel and the 'as required' trip working into the aluminium smelting works at Bloxwich. Ray recalled that when Enterprise was launched in 1994, he was to drive the first train onwards to Bescot when it arrived at Brent, north London. The main train, with a very clean Class 56 in charge, was running so late that Ray was told to take Brent's own contribution to it – just four wagons – on their own to Bescot and he was given a scruffy stand-by Class 31 for the purpose. This did not deter the waiting press photographers as the train left the yard. It was booked to take the fast line, but was signalled onto the slow line, via Northampton. Bescot was still reached on time.

Artists impression of the Alstom-built titling trains for Virgin West Coast. *(courtesy of Alstom)*

Made in Birmingham

Metro-Cammell's contribution to train building since 1973 has been at least as great as at any time in its history. There has been a change of name, first to GEC Alsthom Metro-Cammell, more recently to Alstom.

Major contracts since 1973 have included stock for the Tyne & Wear Metro (1978), the Kowloon-Canton Railway (1979), Mark IV stock for East Coast electrification (1986) and 32 DVTs for the West Coast Main Line (1986). The long tradition of building trains for the London Underground has continued unabated, from the D78 District Line stock of 1976 (75 six-car units) to the 59 six-car units for the Jubilee Line extension (the first in London with wheelchair access) and 106 six-car units to breathe new life into the Northern Line, the last of which left Alstom in March 1999.

In December 1989 the contracts for 31 Eurostar trainsets were placed. Eleven of these enormous 18-car sets were to be assembled at Washwood Heath. They are capable of speeds up to 300kph (186mph) and derive power from three different sources, 750Vdc 3rd rail (England), 25KVac (France and the Tunnel) and 3KVdc (Belgium). Scanning the coach bodies, there is something slightly unfamiliar to the non-technical eye. They are different, but how? The word 'monocoque' probably will not spring to mind, but that is what they are, 'one shell' without a separate chassis. For those wishing to find out more about these superb trains, I recommend "From the Footplate : Eurostar" by Peter Waller (Ian Allan).

Some 14-car North of London (NoL) Eurostars (see page 59) were built here but to date they have not entered service. With hindsight, it was commercially unsound to order 14-car train sets for services linking Glasgow, Manchester and Birmingham with Europe from which domestic passengers within the UK would be excluded. Nevertheless, the NoL sets are high quality products for which a use ought to be found. Their long period of enforced idleness is in no way Alstom's fault. During the summer of 1999 initial high speed test runs were carried out with set 330 by GNER with a view to using some NoL Eurostars on East Coast Main Line domestic services between King's Cross and York ('Rail' issue 363, August 11th 1999)

The Alstom plant in March 1999 was active, busy and – in the words of their Sales Manager – *"operating at the cutting edge of engineering design"*. Three variations of the Juniper electric multiple unit were under construction. Just as there are variables within the same brand name in the motor industry, today's railway builders have become more flexible. The 20metre units are modular, with sliding external plug doors 1/3 and 2/3 of the way along. A customer may opt for air conditioning, various seat layouts, a gangwayed front end or full width cab, etc. *"We can play tunes on it to suit customer requirements, but the base vehicle is a well developed product, so we are taking the risk away from the customer because it is a train where the fundamental mechanicals and electricals have already been proved"*.

South West Trains ordered 30 four coach units (Class 458) to replace slam door stock on the Waterloo-Reading line. Their power source is third rail, but they still have pantograph wells. Porterbrook own and lease them to SWT, so if at some stage they are needed by another lessee for running on 25Kv lines, conversion will be simple. As the SWT units will sometimes need to run in multiple, the ends are gangwayed.

The 8 eight-car Class 460 trains are for Gatwick Express (see page 58).The car at the north end of each train (nearest the buffers at Victoria) is a bonded vehicle for checked-in luggage, which will next be seen by its owners when landing at their final destinations. One quarter of this car is a small business lounge for frequent travellers. Ribbon glazing has been applied to the 460s to give the pleasing external effect of a continuous strip of glazing along each car body. This is glued into position, but as the glue takes hours to set the glazing is also fastened into the body shell, making for a simpler operation when a window needs to be replaced in service. 1¼ cars of the 460s have 2+1 TGV style seating for business class, the remainder of the train has 2+2 seating. Air conditioning plant is housed within the roof space, making the ceiling a little lower (clearance is still more than 2m) but visually the vehicles seem wider. The modular bolt-on cab is not attached during construction, so it can be fitted out easily "through the big hole in the back". If involved in a mishap it can be removed and a spare cab bolted on. The Gatwick Express cab is unmistakable, with a tapered sloping front finishing in a rounded nose, giving it the nickname 'Darth Vader'. Unlike the other two Junipers, the Class 460 has bodyside skirts.

The third Juniper variation is the Class 334 for the Glasgow suburban services of ScotRail, a contract for 40 three-car trains (see page 58). These have two traction motors at each end and a pantograph trailer inbetween. The 334s will allow scrapping of the 305s and the last 303s, the 'Blue trains' of 1959. The first 334 was delivered to Shields Road Depot, Glasgow, on 3rd August 1999.

The bodyshells for SWT and Gatwick Express units were made at the Alstom plant in Barcelona, identical shells for ScotRail originated in Budapest. Their frames are designed to withstand considerable end impact. In the event of a collision there is an 'energy absorption process', in effect a controlled implosion. A very low speed impact will induce the first point of contact, the coupling, merely to bounce. Anything more and the coupling is designed to rip out of its mounting and fall into a cradle, avoiding falling onto the track and derailing the train. The anti-climbers will impact, preventing the vehicles from riding over each other. Anti-climbers are reinforced underframe endings, roughly where traditional buffers used to be. They are ridged, helping them to lock together rather than climb. Just behind them, the underframe has built-in weak points in the form of notches, where any structural collapse should start and be rapidly absorbed. Legal requirements are that the impact design should take out one million joules of energy in the first metre of the vehicle at 100mph. This design is estimated to remove 1.5m joules, making the Juniper extremely safe, even in a high speed collision. In crude terms, the front of the train may be severely bashed, but it should remain on the rails and largely undamaged; passengers will probably be shaken, but should escape serious injury.

For the first time since the Class 156, Alstom resumed building diesel multiple units in 1999. The Class 175 'Coradia' for First Group's North West Trains is a fleet of 11 two-car and 16 three-car 100mph diesel hydraulic units. Alstom maintain the units in service as part of the contract. [This type of 'Design, Build and Maintain' contract, increasingly the norm within the industry, was pioneered by GEC Alsthom with the 1994 Northern Line contract, which includes maintenance for 20 years (see 'Modern Railways' Feb. 1995).] Great effort has gone into designing out noise from each passenger saloon on the 175. The ceiling has special perforations to deflect sound from the roof cavity, the walls are fully insulated and, to deaden the sound of the 450hp Cummins engine, the floor 'floats'. The cavity beneath it eliminates virtually all sound. Interior fittings have to be mounted off the floating floor rather than the wall, to avoid them acting as sound carrying bridges. The first three-car 175 arrived at Kidderminster on 29th/30th July 1999 – by road on three low loaders – for initial testing and running on the Severn Valley Railway (see page 59).

The Class 175 can be used to illustrate the large number of manufacturers based in many countries who combine to build today's trains. The bodyshells came from Barcelona, bogies from France, Cummins engines from Darlington, Voith gearbox from Germany, brake frame from Westinghouse in Chippenham, radiators and gearbox from Coventry, seats from Norway, gangways from Burton-on-Trent, doors from Holland – *"We always try to buy the best kit"*.

All plans are designed and transmitted electronically in solid (3D) model form. There are no paper drawings other than assembly drawings. The Class 175 bodyshell was designed at Washwood Heath and sent electronically to Barcelona. It is possible for the various manufacturers to look at the same solid model on screen simultaneously – a video conference group discussion across Europe. This way of working was used for the first time with the 7 four-car 125mph trains for the Stockholm Airport line, the last of which was virtually complete at the time of my visit.

The Class 180 version of the 'Coradia', for Great Western's HST routes to Bristol, South Wales and the West of England, is designed for 125mph running. These will be the first trains operating at such speed with a passenger compartment in the leading vehicle but agreement with the Railway Inspectorate has to be reached before this can happen. The 180s, with 750hp turbo-charged engines, are designed to absorb 3m joules of energy at full speed impact.

As the last Northern Line train left Washwood Heath its flow line became one of four for the Virgin West Coast tilting trains. There will be 53 train sets and, at £592m, this is the largest ever contract for new trains in the UK, signed on 9th February 1999, a joint venture between Alstom and Fiat Ferroviaria. The contract includes innovative clauses – Alstom and Fiat took responsiblity for the existing West Coast fleet on February 27th to ensure a smooth transition period, and they will be responsible for operating the six train care centres where the new trains will be based. The size of the order is such that Alstom needs to build at a rate of almost two units per day for completion early in 2002. All this is for a different century and beyond my publishing deadline. Meanwhile, there has been considerable revival on the other route to London ....

Two Hours to London

As the 1980s gave way to the 1990s, an ailing local service between London Marylebone and Banbury was being maintained with increasing difficulty by first generation dmus. They were replaced by Class 165 Turbos, which were cascaded into service in the autumn of 1991. Complete modernisation of the route – branded the Chiltern Line – with all new trains, refurbished stations, a computerised signalling system, etc., brought a 15% growth in passengers within a year, making it the most buoyant line on Network South East. NSE and Regional Railways extended half the trains to Birmingham in May 1993, providing a train every two hours between Marylebone and Snow Hill. It was thought that few people would travel end to end because of a journey time of 140+ minutes, but set against this were new trains, with reasonable fares (£19 return) valid even for peak travel. Traffic grew, and trains became hourly in September 1994.

With privatisation the Chiltern Line became Chiltern Railways, a small vibrant company keen to develop its main line further. In the uncertain climate leading up to privatisation no new trains had been built for a British railway for three years, resulting in a period of extreme hardship for some train builders. On 11th September 1996 Chiltern broke the drought and placed an order with Adtranz of Derby – for just four trains! It was greeted with immense relief throughout the industry. The trains were to be 3-car Class 168 Turbostars, with a top speed of 90mph, air conditioning and 2+2 seating of superior comfort, with no first class section. As with the more recent Juniper family of Alstom, these 'Clubman' trains have a bolt-on cab. During construction the 23m aluminium body was inverted to ease installation of the roof fittings. Porterbrook own the trains and lease them to Chiltern. The 165s are limited to 75mph, so the introduction of the 168s meant that key services could run to faster schedules, but not within the constraints of the 26 miles of single track between Aynho and Princes Risborough. Chiltern and Railtrack agreed on a £15m scheme for redoubling the 18 miles south of Bicester. The first Turbostar entered service on 25th May 1998 but the summer time-table could not be introduced until 17th July as the double track was ready but its associated signalling was not. An order was placed for eight

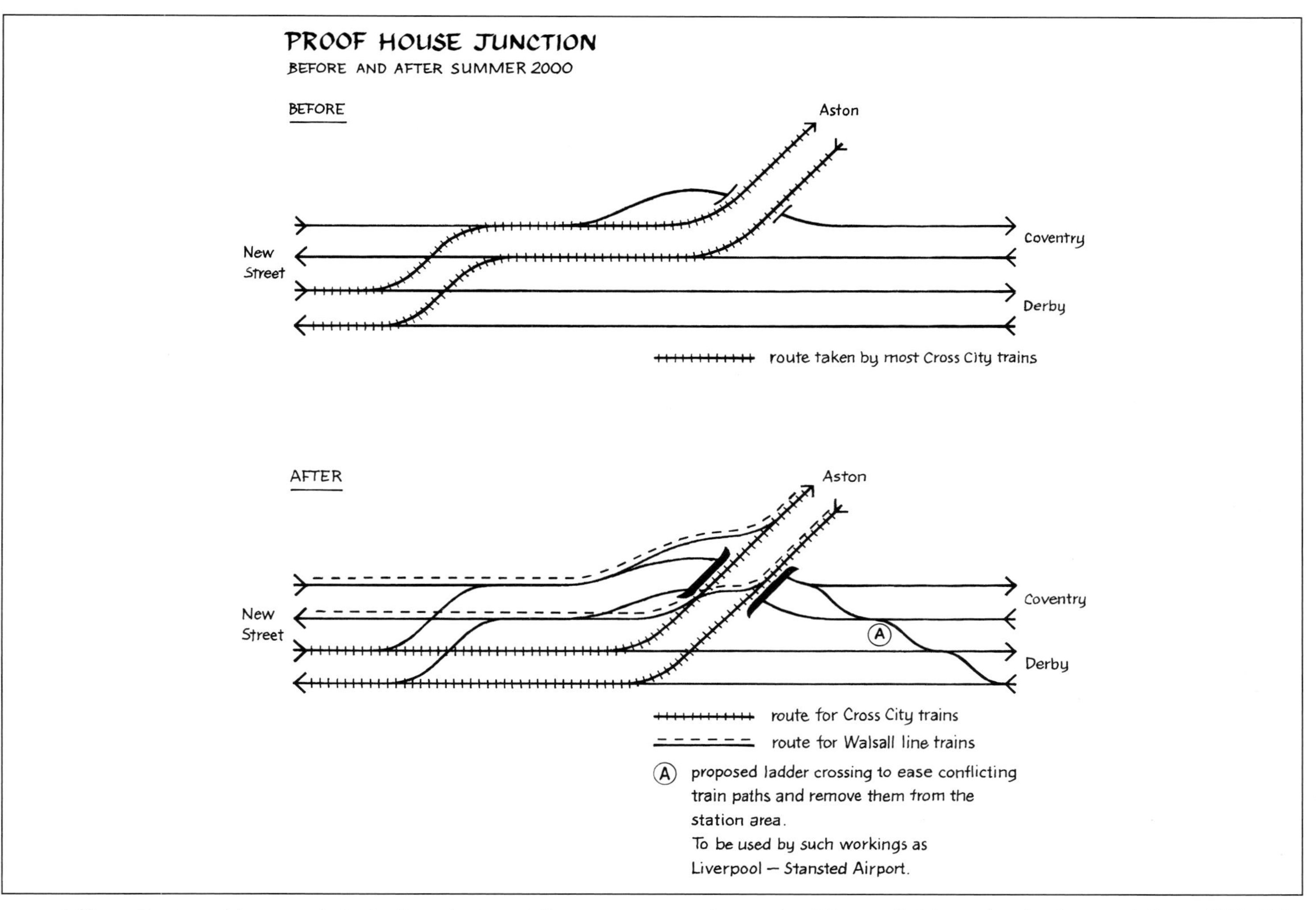

more 168s units, two drivers and six trailers, to turn 4 three-car trains into 5 four-car trains. A further order (April 1999) for 10 driving coaches converts the fleet into 10 three-car trains.

In September 1998 peak services between Snow Hill and Marylebone became half-hourly in response to ever-increasing demand. The fastest Clubmans ran non-stop south of Banbury and completed the journey in 118 minutes, once more bringing Snow Hill within two hours of London. The 1999 summer timetable included stops south of Banbury in all trains, causing timings to be eased to just over two hours.

Chiltern are promoters of the new £3.5m station at Warwick Parkway, 1¼ miles east of the existing Warwick station, close to the A41/A46 intersection, with parking for 400 cars. Central government gave approval for the station in March 1999, attaching the sensible condition that bus operators connecting into the train services must do so for a minimum of five years. At the same time, whilst maintaining that it is keen to see integrated transport, the government walked away from the scheme by refusing to make any financial contribution. No date for completion has been set.

Chiltern fares remain excellent value for money but even on this line peak fares and travel restrictions are increasing. Maybe half a dozen or so seats on every peak train could be available for cheap day return passengers, who would have to make a non-refundable credit card booking the day before. Easy to understand and administer, it could generate considerable goodwill without eroding premium fare revenue.

Since the opening of Midland Metro in May 1999, West Bromwich, Wednesbury and Bilston have all been brought within easier reach of the capital by a simple change at Snow Hill. It is good to see the West Midlands' other route to London very much alive and well, as anyone living in Solihull, Leamington or Warwick will surely agree.

Plans & Schemes

To conclude this final volume of "A Century of Railways", I asked two senior figures within the local railway industry for their thoughts on recent achievements and their hopes for the future.

Until July 1999 Malcolm Keeley was Rail Services Manager at Centro. We began by clarifying the terms West Midlands Passenger Transport Authority (WMPTA), West Midlands Passenger Transport Executive (WMPTE) and Centro.

Under the 1968 Transport Act, responsibility for the operation of local rail services in the largest urban areas outside London – in effect the underwriting of these services' financial losses – was to be transferred from British Rail to newly created passenger transport executives. In 1972 an agreement was signed between WMPTA and the British Railways Board. WMPTA consisted of councillors who, as elected representatives for all the local authorities in the area, thereby assumed responsibility for the loss-making local rail network, as well as the local bus services. To assist these councillors, there are professional officers, collectively known as the WMPTE. This body still exists, but when the local bus services were hived off in 1986 as West Midlands Travel (WMT) for subsequent privatisation, confusion soon followed. As a means of overcoming this the name 'Centro' was coined; Centro is the WMPTE.

Has there been one single development which had brought the greatest benefit for passengers? *"The Cross City Line has got to be the one, because on the south side of Birmingham we went from virtually nothing to a fifteen minute service that was an instant success. I still recollect the opening and being at Longbridge station on the second evening and seeing people pouring off the trains. There were crowds on the overbridge looking down on the incomplete station. In all my transport career I have never seen such numbers of people actually just watching a new transport facility at work. One old chap turned to me and said, 'Well, it's a bit of an advent isn't it?'. Not only was it a magnificent scheme to bring in, but it really had an effect on the public at large, as well as the travelling public."*

The opening of the new Snow Hill in October 1987 re-established a rail presence in an important part of Birmingham city centre. As the new Moor Street was a through station, all local trains from the Leamington and North Warwickshire lines served both Moor Street and Snow Hill for the first time. The completion of the Jewellery Line in 1995, known at the time as 'Snow Hill Phase II', was important because it opened up new areas to rail, created another cross city link and brought welcome relief to New Street, which was able to shed most Stourbridge line trains.

"1994 had been a bad year for local rail services. The industry was being broken up for privatisation and thus in turmoil, and there had been a signalling strike. A long period of disruption during Cross City electrification was followed by an unreliable service, maintained with difficulty by a mixture of heritage diesels and old Class 304 and 308 emus. Late delivery of the purpose-built 323s was compounded by protracted teething troubles once they entered service. 1995 turned a corner, as the time-tables were tweaked and the 323s at last proved capable of running a reliable and punctual Cross City service. Then the Jewellery Line opened in September, with three new stations. Not only did it relieve some of the pressure on New Street, but the overall effect was to improve punctuality for all local lines, both at New Street and Snow Hill."

The stock and train crew saved when the Jewellery Line opened permitted an increased frequency on the Shirley line from two to three trains an hour, and on the Walsall line from three to four trains an hour, plus extra peak trains to Stourbridge. *"This is a classic example of taking the same amount of resources and re-using them in a different way."*

All local rail services make a financial loss, but the PTA has always appreciated their value in moving people around the West Midlands. The authority is consistently supportive of rail. There has been, over the years, an 'acceptable level of resource', which has been fluid. *"I can remember poaching the odd train from one line at the peak and giving it to another because I felt that the time-table development could stand it – and it did."* New types of stock often have more seats than the equivalent 'heritage' units and they are faster. Stock can also be saved when trains do not have to spend time turning round at New Street or Snow Hill. They run through, a saving in train crews and the number of trains themselves. The PTA has not pursued a policy of cutting back on rail and has always welcomed the opportunity of re-using resources without increasing them where possible.

New Street is seen as the hub of both the national and local rail network, but also as something of a bogeyman. It is a major bottleneck, with the number of daily train movements (around 840) greater than ever and demand for more services continuing. Much of the spare capacity created when the Jewellery Line opened has been used up again. *"In the early days of privatisation, Railtrack – inexperienced at the new game, like all the other players – was a little over-eager to sell train paths to private operators, who have franchise plans to adhere to and who need to build up new business. That doesn't mean to say that New Street can't take extra trains"*, said Malcolm, challenging a popular notion. *"The important thing is what those trains do when they get to New Street and whether they have to cross many tracks to get out of the other side, but it certainly is not that difficult to fit extra trains into and out of the station, provided they are performing simple manoeuvres. More trains making manoeuvres which are less straightforward, however, will require substantial investment. The remodelling of Proof House Junction, during the summer of 2000, is designed to ease this difficult location and involves a total shutdown of the junction for several weeks."*

Centro has issued a new Twenty Year Strategy, identifying areas where it would like to see further improvements. There are hopes for 'turn-up-and-go' services on some routes, with a ten minute frequency. Candidates include Longbridge-Four Oaks and the Walsall Line. A strong case for both these services can be made if they are also improved in other ways, bringing benefits to the whole line. More people will use Longbridge-Four Oaks, for instance, if the branch to Frankley is re-opened and electrified, and if some Cross City trains are sent down an electrified Lickey to terminate at Bromsgrove. Electrification between Walsall and Rugeley would enhance the whole line, converting the route to faster emus and eliminating the mix of rolling stock on the Walsall line. It would mean that all tracks through the Walsall station bottleneck would be electrified. It would also be of benefit if Birmingham-Walsall trains were extended to Aldridge, or to Wolverhampton, with a new station at Willenhall. (Railtrack's Network Management Statement mentions electrification of Walsall-Rugeley and the Sutton Park Line.) The Walsall trains which use the Soho Loop could call at the proposed new station at the International Convention Centre.

"Probably the knottiest problem will be the Walsall-Stourbridge-Dudley Line. The Black Country consists of relatively small communities. Its lines of communication need to serve a lot of places, so dual running of rail and Midland Metro needs active consideration as the Metro can get into the centre of Dudley and Merry Hill."

Another problem is electrification of the Snow Hill group of lines. There are few obvious termini. Stourbridge-Dorridge is the core of the route, but if you electrify to Stourbridge, why not to Kidderminster, or Worcester? If to Dorridge, why not to Leamington and Shirley, or Stratford? In short - where do you stop?

The Camp Hill Line is Birmingham's forgotten rail route – *"Its hard to think of a corridor that cries out more for a rail based turn-up-and-go service"* but constraints on the route, particularly into a central Birmingham terminus, mean that any stations on the line are unlikely in the near future.

A further problem for the early years of the new century will be the biggest bottleneck of all - the Birmingham-Coventry Line, which urgently needs extra track capacity, but so far *"Railtrack are looking to others rather than leading the way on this one"*.

These problems, although real, are caused by growth in rail traffic. *"For the early part of my transport career we were looking at contraction, now we are looking at continued growth. We are nowhere near exhausting the potential demand for local rail services – I can't tell you what a positive pleasure that is!"*

It is not always easy to understand how the privatised railway system works. Mike Haigh, Head of Performance and Planning at Central Trains, offered an explanation. Birmingham based Central Trains (CT) is part of the National Express Group (NEX) and one of five NEX Train Operating Companies (TOCs). Altogether there are 25 passenger TOCs across the country.

On the congested Stour Valley Line, 86 101 "Sir William A.Stanier FRS" heads past the site of Winson Green station with the 10.40 Euston-Shrewsbury on 6th December 1986. The bridge carries Dudley Road over Telford's double towpathed 'main line' canal. Through its arch is an abutment of the bridge that once carried the Harborne Railway. *(John Whitehouse)*

Central Trains have a seven year franchise, from March 1997 to April 2004, which allows them to operate trains and collect revenue. *"We pay track access charges to Railtrack, we lease rolling stock, we manage drivers, conductors and our own station staff."* CT have 2,300 staff and a network of services stretching across a broad band of the country, from Pwllheli to Skegness and East Anglia. Company turnover is £260m per annum. The business is a broad portfolio, ranging from express services between cities, to urban commuter services and rural services. The franchise subsidy in 1997 was £173m, falling to £130m by 2004. As the subsidy reduces so the business must grow – *"It was very clear at the outset that what we are about is growth".*

"It is generally recognised that CT and Centro enjoy one of the best relationships between an operator and a PTE". Centro sets the specification for the level of train services and fares in its area and Central Trains operates those services, as part of the franchise agreement.

The two years from March 1997 saw a 20% growth in passenger revenue on Central Trains. The biggest increase (30%) was on the Norwich-Liverpool route, through Nottingham, Sheffield and Manchester. There was significant growth on the Birmingham-Stansted Airport route, which has become marginally profitable, due in part to a rapid growth in airport traffic. When the Cambridge-Stansted section was all but abandoned by Regional Railways in 1994, it was losing £1m a year. Numbers of passengers using the Coventry/Birmingham-Leicester-Lincoln services grew from 122,000 for a four week period in Jan/Feb 1998 to 136,000 for the same period in 1999, up 11.4%. Growth on the Birmingham-Shrewsbury-Aberystwyth/Chester lines *"is such that we are crowded even in the off-peak and we are evaluating further frequency improvements between Wolverhampton, Shrewsbury and Chester".*

Within the West Midlands commuting markets are strong. Passenger numbers are growing to the extent that predictions implicit in the franchise have become inadequate. It was thought that 112 units (ie; 'coaches' not whole trainsets) would be sufficient for Centro's anticipated peak hour traffic by 2004, *"but we are there now and traffic is still growing; we have a problem, or rather, we have an opportunity",* so CT and Centro are looking at ways of providing extra trains and creating more capacity.

The Class 170 dmus, built by Adtranz at Derby and leased to Central Trains, are in two builds. Thirteen 2-car sets, with 122 seats, air-conditioning and a maximum speed of 100mph, enter service in 1999, with ten 3-car sets and ten 2-car sets to follow in 2000. *"These orders were not part of our franchise commitment",* said Mike, *"we didn't have to do it, but it is now essential to provide capacity for growth".* The 2-car sets are for the routes from Birmingham to Stansted, Liverpool and Aberystwyth; the 3-car sets are for the Cardiff-Birmingham-Nottingham and Norwich-Liverpool routes. The introduction of this new stock into service, which began on 29th July 1999, enables trains to run at improved frequencies on the core routes, easing overcrowding. It will also affect other routes, enabling the last slam door Class 310 emus to be replaced by 323s from the Birmingham-Liverpool route when – as seems likely – the Class 170s run a through Liverpool-Birmingham-Stansted service.

Central Trains' new livery, launched in 1999, is a bold two-tone green, complete with the company's Telesales phone number writ large. *"It says, we are here, we have an identity to be proud of",* suggested Mike. The bright shade of blue applied to the roof extends down the sides of the driving cab. It is to be applied to all trains except those in existing Centro livery, which cannot be changed without Centro's agreement. Since 1997 Central Trains

Along the severely congested Birmingham-Coventry line, a down Virgin West Coast train hurtles past the 1839 buildings of the Birmingham & Derby Junction station at Hampton-in-Arden, 29th April 1999. *(John Boynton)*

have run a successful advertising campaign, most visible on local television, where a twenty second slot displayed the company's core routes, highlighted some bargain fares and finished with the slogan – delivered in a mock upper crust voice – "Central Trains – GO!!!". Another easily remembered phrase was "Central Trains – Central to your journey". Fares were promoted for 'Under a Fiver' and 'Under a Tenner' (eg; cheap day returns Birmingham-Stratford £3.50, Coventry-Nottingham £8.10, Warwick-Shrewsbury £8.20). Central Trains are now concentrating their advertising campaigns on individual routes and, in particular, off-peak travel. With an overall load factor of 35%, there are still plenty of seats to fill.

The biggest single issue facing Central Trains, and all other train operating companies, is the capacity of the network and its ability to handle ever increasing amounts of traffic. There is concern within the industry that congestion at the 'pinch points' will not be adequately resolved and that a brake will be put on growth to match the existing infrastructure, instead of expanding the infrastructure to accommodate growth. While capacity remains scarce it may have to be rationed. If, for instance, Virgin were to be allowed sufficient train paths between Birmingham and Coventry to double the frequency of its Euston service, without the provision of extra tracks, this would have serious implications for other operators on the route. Their services could be reduced in frequency and they would be expected to meet the costs of additional tracks at some future date.

On the approaches to New Street from the Coventry end there is (at the time of writing) a debate about whether to provide an extra pair of tracks between Proof House Junction and the station. It would be expensive (it would also be an investment!) but there is room on the south side of the cuttings/tunnels if the cut and cover method were to be adopted and if work were to be carried out in conjuction with the redevelopment of the adjacent Bull Ring area.

Capacity problems between Birmingham and Wolverhampton have serious implications for the proposed new station at the International Convention Centre and for developing the role of Galton Bridge as an interchange station. There just isn't the time available between trains to allow many services to call there. Extra tracks, or even the simple upgrading of the existing freight loops to passenger standard, would ease the pressure. Similarly, the single track section between Coventry and Leamington has negative implications for the development of local services along that route and the construction of a station at Kenilworth.

As more trains are squeezed along existing tracks, performance drops and services will run to slower timings as recovery time increases, a classic symptom of rail congestion. As yet, Railtrack does not appear to have sufficient will to provide the extra capacity. Hopefully, the new Strategic Rail Authority is a body that will have teeth. Whether regionally or nationally, it needs to view the rail network as an integrated whole, so that the costs of improvements will be spread fairly and the benefits will be felt by all users.

As the whole rail system grows, in the West Midlands as elsewhere, the challenge of growing it smoothly – to satisfy commuters, long distance travellers, freight users, environmentalists, etc – is one that will exercise the minds of those within the industry for many years to come.

STATION GAZETTEER

This gazetter includes the names of stations, opening and closure dates to passenger traffic, other names, etc. Two sets of dates indicate opening, closure and re-opening (eg; Stourbridge Town), sometimes followed by final closure (eg; Princes End). Where no closure date is given, the station has been continuously open to passengers on the same or a similar site. Station which have opened or reopened since 1972 are starred *.

ACOCKS GREEN 1852 (renamed 'Acocks Green & South Yardley' in 1878, now 'Acocks Green' again)
ADDERLEY PARK 1860
ALBION 1853-1960
ALDRIDGE 1879-1965
ALVECHURCH 1859
ASTON 1854
BAPTIST END 1905-1964
BARNT GREEN 1840
BERKSWELL 1844 (opened as Docker's Lane, Berkswell 1853, Berkswell & Balsall Common 1882, now reverted to Berkswell.)
BESCOT 1847 (now BESCOT STADIUM)
BILSTON CENTRAL 1854-1972 ('Central' added in 1950)
BILSTON WEST 1854-1962 ('West' added in 1950)
BIRCHILLS 1858-1916
* BIRMINGHAM INTERNATIONAL 1976
* BIRMINGHAM MOOR ST. 1909-1987 (terminus replaced by present through stn. in 1987)
BIRMINGHAM NEW ST. 1851 (temporary stn.for local service to Wolverhampton) 1854 (main stn.)
* BIRMINGHAM SNOW HILL 1852-1972 : 1987
BLACKWELL 1840-1965
BLAKEDOWN 1852 (formerly CHURCHILL, then CHURCHILL & BLAKEDOWN)
BLAKE ST. 1884
BLOWERS GREEN 1878-1962 (named 'Dudley (South Side) & Netherton before 1921)
BLOXWICH 1858-1965 (in Station Street)
* BLOXWICH 1989 (new station in Croxdene Avenue, north of the original)
* BLOXWICH NORTH 1990 (situated at Broad Lane)
BORDESLEY 1855
BOURNVILLE 1876 (earlier known as STIRCHLEY ST. and STIRCHLEY ST.& BOURNVILLE)
BRADLEY & MOXLEY 1862-1915 (site near today's Bradley Lane Metro stop)
BRETTELL LANE 1852-1962
BRIERLEY HILL 1858-1962
BRIGHTON ROAD 1875-1941
BRINDLEY HEATH 1939-1959
BROCKMOOR HALT 1925-1932
BROMFORD BRIDGE 1896-1965 (racecourse stn., served only by specials)
BROMLEY HALT 1925-1932
BROMSGROVE 1840
BROWNHILLS (Midland) 1884-1930
BROWNHILLS (LNWR) 1849-1965
BUSHBURY 1852-1912
* BUTLER'S LANE 1957-1991 : 1992 (new station on same site)
CAMP HILL 1841-1941
CANLEY 1940
* CANNOCK 1859-1965 : 1989 (new station on same site)
CASTLE BROMWICH 1842-1968
CHESTER ROAD 1863
CHURCH ROAD 1876-1925
COLESHILL 1839-1916 remained open for goods and renamed MAXSTOKE IN 1923
(see also Forge Mills)
COMPTON HALT 1925-1932
COOMBES HOLLOWAY HALT 1905-1927
COSELEY 1902 (replaced Deepfields, opened 1852, 400 metres to north)
COVENTRY 1838
CRADLEY HEATH 1863 (earlier known as Cradley Heath & Cradley)
CUTNALL GREEN HALT 1928-1965
DAISY BANK 1854-1916 : 1919-1962
DANZEY 1908 (opened as Danzey for Tanworth)
DARBY END 1905-1964
DARLASTON 1837-1965 (known by various combinations of the words 'Darlaston' and 'James Bridge' until 1913, when the name was fixed by request of Darlaston Urban District Council)
DORRIDGE 1852 (see KNOWLE)
DROITWICH 1852 (known as DTOITWICH SPA since 1923)
DUDLEY 1850-1964
DUDLEY PORT (Stour Valley platforms) 1852
DUDLEY PORT (South Staffordshire Line platforms) 1850-1964
DUNSTALL PARK 1896-1916 : 1919-1968
EARLSWOOD 1908 (formerly Earlswood Lakes)
ERDINGTON 1862
ETTINGSHALL ROAD 1852-1964
* FIVE WAYS 1885-1944 : 1978
FOLESHILL 1850-1965
FORGE MILLS 1842-1965 (renamed COLESHILL in 1923)
FOUR OAKS 1884
GORNAL HALT 1925-1932
GRAVELLY HILL 1862
GREAT BRIDGE (NORTH) 1850-1964 ('North' added 1950)
GREAT BRIDGE (SOUTH) 1866-1915 : 1920-1964 ('South' added 1950)
GREAT WYRLEY 1858-1965 (also known as Wyrley & Cheslyn Hay)
GRIMES HILL & WYTHALL 1908 (opened as Grimes Hill Platform, now named WYTHALL)
HAGLEY opening date uncertain, first appeared in timetables in 1862
HAGLEY ROAD 1874-1934
HALESOWEN 1878-1927 (open until 1960 for workmen's trains)
HALL GREEN 1908
HAMMERWICH 1849-1965
HAMPTON-IN-ARDEN (LNWR) 1837 (stn.moved 1/4 mile south-east to present site, 1884)
HAMPTON-IN-ARDEN (MR branch from Whitacre) 1839-1916
HAMSTEAD 1862 (formerly GREAT BARR)
HANDSWORTH & SMETHWICK 1854-1972
HANDSWORTH WOOD 1896-1941
HARBORNE 1874-1934
HARTLEBURY 1852
HARTS HILL 1895-1916
HATTON 1852
HAZELWELL 1903-1941
HEATH TOWN 1872-1910
* HEDNESFORD 1859-1965 : 1989
HENLEY-IN-ARDEN (branch terminus) 1894-1908
HENLEY-IN-ARDEN (North Warwickshire Line) 1908
HIMLEY 1925-1932
HOCKLEY 1854-1972 (site is west of the present Jewellery Quarter stn.)
HUNNINGTON 1883-1919 (stn.sidings served the Bluebird toffee factory)
ICKNIELD PORT ROAD 1874-1931
* JEWELLERY QUARTER 1995
KENILWORTH 1844-1965
KIDDERMINSTER 1852
* KIDDERMINSTER TOWN (SVR) 1984
KINGSBURY 1839-1965
KINGS HEATH 1840-1941 (known as MOSELEY before 1867)
KINGS NORTON 1849
KNOWLE & DORRIDGE 1852 ('& Dorridge' added in 1899, now named DORRIDGE)
* LANDYWOOD 1908-1916 : 1989 (new station with staggered platforms)
LANGLEY GREEN 1885
LAPWORTH 1854 (known as KINGSWOOD until 1902)
LEA HALL 1939
LEAMINGTON SPA 1852 ('Spa' not added until 1913)
LEAMINGTON SPA AVENUE 1844-1965
LICHFIELD CITY 1849
LICHFIELD TRENT VALLEY 1847 (Trent Valley Line platforms)
* LICHFIELD TRENT VALLEY 1849-1965 : 1988 (high level platforms, replaced by one new platform on electrification of the Cross City Line)
LIFFORD 1885-1941 (third station)
LONGBRIDGE 1915-1960 (stn.on Halesowen branch, workmen's services only)
* LONGBRIDGE 1978 (Cross City station)
LYE 1863 (no station in Britain has a shorter name)
MARSTON GREEN 1844
MILVERTON 1844-1965 (opened as 'Leamington', underwent several name changes which included the words 'Warwick', 'Leamington' and 'Milverton' in various combinations)
MONMORE GREEN 1863-1916
MONUMENT LANE 1854-1958
MOSELEY 1867-1941
NEWTON ROAD 1837-1945
NORTHFIELD 1870
NORTH WALSALL 1872-1925
OCKER HILL 1864-1890 : 1895-1916
OLDBURY (LNWR main line) 1852
(replaced on same site by SANDWELL & DUDLEY in 1983 without interruption to train service)
OLDBURY (GWR branch terminus) 1885-1916
OLD HILL 1866
OLD HILL HIGH ST. HALT 1905-1964
OLTON 1869
PELSALL 1849-1965
PENN HALT 1925-1932
PENNS 1879-1965
PENSNETT HALT 1925-1932
PERRY BARR 1837 (the present station is on the same site as the Grand Junction Railway original)
PLECK 1881-1917 : 1924-1958
PRIESTFIELD 1854-1962 (Wolverhampton-Worcester line platforms)
PRIESTFIELD 1854-1972 (Wolverhampton-Birmingham line platforms)
Stn.site on curve, just south of Priestfield stop on the Metro.
PRINCES END 1863-1890 : 1895-1916
PRINCES END & COSELEY 1853-1962 ('& Coseley' added in 1936)
REDDITCH 1859 (current stn. is fourth; second stn. 1868-1974; third 1974-1993)
ROTTON PARK ROAD 1874-1934
ROUND OAK 1852-1962 (known as 'Brierley Hill & Round Oak' before 1857)
ROWLEY REGIS 1867
RUBERY 1883-1919
* RUGELEY TOWN 1870-1965 : 1997 (south of original station)
RUGELEY TRENT VALLEY 1847
RUSHALL 1849-1909 (first station in the West Midlands to close in the twentieth century)
SALTLEY 1854-1968
* SANDWELL & DUDLEY 1983 (InterCity station on the site of Oldbury)
SELLY OAK 1876
SHENSTONE 1884
SHIRLEY 1908
SHORT HEATH (Clark's Lane) 1872-1931
SMALL HEATH 1863 (opened as 'Small Heath & Sparkbrook')
* SMETHWICK GALTON BRIDGE 1995
SMETHWICK ROLFE STREET 1852
SMETHWICK WEST 1867-1996 (formerly known as Smethwick Junction)
SOLIHULL 1852
SOHO (LNWR) 1867-1949
SOHO (GWR) 1854-1972 (known as Soho & Winson Green from 1893)
SOHO ROAD 1889-1941
SOMERSET ROAD 1876-1930
SPON LANE 1852-1960
SPRING ROAD 1908 (opened as Spring Road Platform)
STECHFORD 1844 (replaced by stn. on present site in 1882)
STOKE WORKS 1852-1965
STOURBRIDGE JUNCTION 1852 (present station and junction, south of earlier, opened 1901)
STOURBRIDGE TOWN 1879-1915 : 1919
STREETLY 1879-1965
SUTTON COLDFIELD 1862
SUTTON PARK 1879-1965
SUTTON TOWN 1879-1924
SWAN VILLAGE 1854-1972
* TAME BRIDGE PARKWAY 1990
TETTENHALL 1925-1932
THE HAWTHORNS 1931-1968 (served only by football specials)
* THE HAWTHORNS 1995
THE LAKES 1935 (opened as The Lakes Halt)
TILE HILL 1864
TIPTON FIVE WAYS 1853-1962 ('Five Ways' added in 1950)
TIPTON OWEN ST. 1852 ('Owen St.' added, 1950-62)
TYSELEY 1906
* UNIVERSITY 1978
VAUXHALL 1869 (also known as VAUXHALL & DUDDESTON, now known as DUDDESTON)
WALSALL 1847
WALSALL WOOD 1884-1930
WARWICK 1852
WATER ORTON 1842
WEDNESBURY CENTRAL 1854-1972 ('Central' added in 1950)
WEDNESBURY TOWN 1850-1964 ('Town' added in 1950)

WEDNESFIELD 1872-1931
WEST BROMWICH 1854-1972
WHITACRE 1842-1968 (stn. on junction site after 1864)
WHITLOCK'S END 1936-1999 : 1999 (new station on same site)
WIDNEY MANOR 1899
WILLENHALL 1837-1965
WILLENHALL STAFFORD ST. 1872-1931
WINDMILL END 1878-1964
WINSON GREEN 1876-1957
WITTON 1876
WOLVERHAMPTON HIGH LEVEL 1852 (known as 'Wolverhampton' 1852-1853 and since 1972; 'Wolverhampton Queen St.' 1853-1885 and 'Wolverhampton High Level' 1885-1972)
WOLVERHAMPTON LOW LEVEL 1854-1972 ('Low Level' added in 1856)
WOMBOURN 1925-1932
WOOD END 1908 (opened as Wood End Platform)
WOOD GREEN 1881-1941 (also known as Wood Green [Old Bescot])
WYLDE GREEN 1862
YARDLEY WOOD 1908 (opened as Yardley Wood Platform)

WEST MIDLAND STATIONS WHICH CLOSED BEFORE 1900
(excluding stations replaced without a break on the same or a similar site)

BENTLEY 1872-1898 (on MR Walsall-Wolverhampton Line, between North Walsall and Short Heath - closure due to tramway competition)
BESCOT BRIDGE 1837-1850 (Wood Green opened on same site 1881)
BIRMINGHAM CURZON STREET (Grand Junction Rly.) 1839-1854
BIRMINGHAM CURZON STREET (London & Birmingham Rly.) 1838-1854 (used by some excursion trains until 1893)
BIRMINGHAM GRANVILLE STREET 1876-1885 (terminus of the Birmingham West Suburban Rly. – Granville Street is off Broad Street – station closed when Midland Rly. main line extended into New Street via Five Ways)
BIRMINGHAM LAWLEY STREET (Birmingham & Derby Junction Rly.) 1842-1851 (trains diverted to Curzon St.)
BLOOMSBURY & NECHELS 1856-1869 (south of Aston)
BROMFORD FORGE 1842-1843 (same site as Bromford Bridge racecourse station)
DARLASTON 1863-1887 (station on the Darlaston Loop Line)
LIFFORD 1840-1844 (second station not open until 1876)
LONGBRIDGE 1840-1849 (on the main line on a similar site to the present station – special station on main line for hospital trains during WWI – station on the Halesowen branch for car workers, 1915-1960 - no public station at Longbridge between 1849 and 1978)
PORTOBELLO 1854-1873 (at junction of GJ and LNW east of Wolverhampton)
ROOD END 1867-1885 (closed when LANGLEY GREEN opened – road at level crossing south of Langley Green is still Station Road, marking the site of Rood End)
RYDER'S HAYS 1856-1858 (north of Pelsall)
VAUXHALL 1837-1839 or 1840 – temporary terminus of the Grand Junction Railway before completion of their Curzon St. station and its approach viaduct.
WOLVERHAMPTON (Grand Junction Rly.) 1837-1852 (re-opened as Wednesfield Heath 1853, closed 1853-55, closed permanently 1873)
WOLVERHAMPTON STAFFORD ROAD (Shrewsbury & Birmingham Rly.) 1850-1854

ACKNOWLEDGEMENTS

Many people have readily offered help, advice, assistance, use of facilities, photographs, etc. in the preparation of this book. Particular thanks are due to the following –

Anna Burke – Birmingham Post librarian
Ray Churchill – railwayman
Graeme Clark – Alstom Transport Ltd.
Michael Denholm – archive material
Mike Haig – Central Trains
Vaughan Heath – Centro
Colin Hunt – Lawley Street Freightliner Terminal
Robert Jones – Birmingham Railway Museum
Malcolm Keeley – Centro
Simon Mole – Railtrack, Birmingham
Maurice Newman – railwayman
Robert Pearson – archive material
David Postle – Kidderminster Railway Museum
Alun Rees – Severn Valley Railway
Jane Rogers – Alstom Transport Ltd.
Ron Swift – Bromsgrove
David Webb – Hams Hall Freight Terminal
Ken Werrett – proof reading

Some of the above provided photographs, as did the following – R.G.Amott, Andrew Bell, John Edgington, Michael Mensing, Brian Moone, David Paggett, Alan Searle, Roger Shenton, Bob Sweet, C.C. Thorburn, John Whitehouse, Terry Walsh, Stephen Widdowson.

The author wishes to state that although he received much valuable assistance from railway staff and others working in an official capacity, any unattributable opinions expressed in the text of this book are entirely his own.

BIBLIOGRAPHY

(and related reading)

A PICTORIAL RECORD OF BRITISH RAILWAYS DIESEL MULTIPLE UNITS
Brian Golding : Cheona Publications : 1995 : ISBN 1 900298 00 7

A REGIONAL HISTORY OF THE RAILWAYS OF GREAT BRITAIN
Volume 7, The West Midlands
Rex Christiansen : David & Charles : 1973 : ISBN 07153 6093 0

BRITISH RAIL OPERATIONS IN THE 1980s
Colin Marsden : Oxford Publishing Co. : 1983 : ISBN 0 86093 248 6

FROM THE FOOTPLATE : EUROSTAR
Peter Waller : Ian Allan : 1998 : ISBN 0 7110 2427 8

PAST AND PRESENT, THE WEST MIDLANDS
John Whitehouse & Geoff Dowling : Past & Present Publishing : 1994 : ISBN 1 85895 075 9

RAIL CENTRES; WOLVERHAMPTON
Paul Collins : Ian Allan Ltd. : 1990 : ISBN 0 7110 1892 8

RAILWAYS OF THE WEST MIDLANDS, A CHRONOLOGY
Charles Clinker : Stephenson Locomotive Society : 1954

WEST MIDLANDS RAILS IN THE 1980s
John Glover : Ian Allan Ltd. : 1984 : ISBN 0 7110 1354 3

Various journals, newspapers and documents, particularly "Modern Railways", all acknowledged within the text.